The Embryonic World Church

Stephen R. Gohr, BRE, ThD

PublishAmerica
Baltimore

First printing

At the specific preference of the author, PublishAmerica allowed this work to remain exactly as the author intended, verbatim, without editorial input.

All scripture quotations are from the King James Version of the Holy Bible.

ISBN: 1-4241-8297-2
PUBLISHED BY PUBLISHAMERICA, LLLP
www.publishamerica.com
Baltimore

Printed in the United States of America

Dedication

This book is dedicated to my three children, Lisa Ruth Gohr Harman, Stephen Robert Gohr and Lyne Rebecca Gohr Kohr, who grew up with the blessings and trials of being Pastor's Kids!

Acknowledgments

This book is the result of many years of study. Originally much of it was written for a thesis which was required in earning my Doctorate of Theology. Each chapter has been encouraged by people in my congregations and the teaching they received during my twenty-five plus years as a pastor. It is comforting to know that there are many who share what this book is all about. I am especially thankful to you who have advanced the ideas that backed up the crucial convictions included herein.

Those who proofread and gave me suggestions have in every way been a vital part in the development of this work. The hours of preparation by my wife on the computer doing things I could never do have been a godsend and blessing. Thank you my darling Carolyne. Thanks also to my son-in-law Troy Harman, a National Park Ranger and historian, for his advice in world events and trends. Thanks also to each one in our home Bible study groups who offered opinions and support, which helped, shape this book.

But most important I thank you my Great God and your Holy Spirit for enlightening me. I give you all the praise.

Contents

Preface

The days of man are brief, *"as a vapor that appeareth for a little time, then vanisheth away."* It must be realized that life is temporary—that is life here and now in this earthly realm, whether it be "*three score and ten; or if by reason of strength, fourscore years.*" Then *"it is appointed unto men once to die, but after this the judgment."*

These quotes from the Bible are mentioned for those who live unto themselves, caring not of the things or the days to come, and one purpose of this book is to warn such ones that the plan of Almighty God is being worked out—a plan that will include great days of horror and devastation on this world. This author truly believes that these very days are at our doorstep now. Every effort has been made to clearly explain these events in a concise manner.

It has been over twenty years now since this book was first begun. It had an urgency then and has much more of an urgency now. Since then we have seen the World Trade Center crumble to dust, the anthrax scare, Afghanistan, Iraq, North Korea, child abuse by hundreds of Roman Catholic priests, the space shuttle fragmenting, the recognition of homosexual marriages and unions, the Euro monetary system and a whole slew of historical events—literally history in the making. Things that we could not even imagine have become reality.

Remember—after you have read this book and have been made aware of God's truth, you will be held responsible. Every man, woman and child must know of the future that God has given in the prophetical portions of His Word. Please carefully and prayerfully read "THE EMBRYONIC WORLD CHURCH" and then share it with someone that you love.

Introduction

By the time this book goes to press it may already be too late. Nevertheless it is still expedient that we proceed and hope that perchance the Lord might tarry His return a little longer. The reason is indeed critical, because many who are caught up unknowingly in the dilemma of forming a one-world church should be enlightened about this most crucial matter. They must withdraw from any such groups, organizations, or systems which are either directly or indirectly playing the pawns, to make the masses of humanity conform to Satan's subtle plan of deception for this age.

God's timetable for the ages cannot be averted and His eternal sovereign plan will definitely come about. Included in His plan, based upon the authority of the infallible Word of God, is the eventual formation of a global, political, economic, and religious system, headed by one man—the Antichrist (Revelation 13-15). I John 2:18, which was written almost two thousand years ago, indicates that certain evil elements existed even then and surfaced from time to time. These destructive forces brought havoc, destruction and death to countless millions of inhabitants of earth. We read: "*Little children, it is the last time; and as ye have heard that Antichrist shall come, even now are there many antichrists, by which we know that it is the last time.*" Certainly if the Apostle John writing under the inspiration of the Holy Spirit of God considered it to be the last time, it would seem most logical, in analyzing the situation, that today we are indeed drastically closer than ever before to the full manifestation of Antichrist and his one-world church.

It is my hope that you will prayerfully read this book and then evaluate your present condition and position of Christian life and service. Look at your own church to see if she falls within the spectrum of compromise, weakened doctrines or unity with outright apostates. Then withdraw yourself if need be so that you will not become a partaker of her evil deeds.

This book may be very shocking to many, while to others it is only the icing on the cake in showing that salvation draweth nigh. Read carefully and with an open and understanding heart. If the possibilities presented in this book are true (and there is every reason to believe they are) it may be worthwhile for you to seek spiritual insight and wisdom from on high in these critical last days.

1
The Decay of History

There is certainly much room for thought and conjecture when reviewing historical events and antiquity, especially in this helter-skelter world. Mankind never seems to learn, especially in the spiraling whirlpool of depraved minds. The world has already seen Antichrist at work in Nero, Hitler and countless other tyrants. These despots, dictatorial and merciless, only foreshadow as types the authentic man of sin himself, Anti-christ, and his eventual reign in global affairs and the establishment, for a short stay, of his one-world church.

Fortunately, nothing happens by chance. Our sovereign God brings about everything exactly and in perfect harmony with his own design. If God ceased to exist the world would cease to exist. It is as simple as that. There are certain things that God may wink at now, but eventually the great day of reckoning will arrive. The tens of thousands of early martyrs who were thrown to the lions, mutilated at the hands of gladiators, beheaded by the guillotine, burned at the stake, asphyxiated in gas chambers, will all be avenged.

Yes, the of spirit of Antichrist is already at work and has been for thousands of years. The same Antichrist who threw the world into the dark ages when a type of world church existed will once more briefly become predominant in world affairs (Revelation 13:11). As was mentioned earlier, nothing is really new. Review this dark period of time. Nothing could be undertaken apart from approval of Holy Mother Church. If one stated that the earth was round and not flat, or that the earth revolved around the sun instead of vice versa, or especially discovered that man could be justified by faith apart from works and the church, he would be anathematized and condemned. It was recently brought to our attention that the Vatican might soon recant on Galileo's condemnation as a heretic in 1616 for teaching that the earth revolved around the sun. The Vatican has never revoked Galileo's conviction as a heretic.

If the patterns hold true regarding history repeating itself, do not be surprised when the aforesaid things happen again in a modern dark age called "The Tribulation."

May it also be mentioned that one prime ingredient which compelled the world to take the course of darkness was an absence of God's Word, the Bible. It was placed on the list of forbidden books and taken away from the laity in the year 1229 A.D. by the Council of Valencia. Along with this came the emergence of a conquering attitude in the name of Christ, imposing so-called Christian standards on barbarian peoples. These defeated peoples were compelled by the conquerors to participate in massive baptisms and were incorporated into the church bringing with them pagan practices that still abound today. Jesus never taught salvation by force in building His church. Later in this book a list of Roman inventions will be given, so that you might become aware of what has taken place in times past and what is yet to come in the future.

Is it any wonder that the world was plunged into darkness?

A Papal system was born, which instituted the wearing of clerical garb that was fashioned straight from another type of Antichrist, Pharaoh. By aligning themselves into a hierarchy of Pope, Cardinals, Bishops and Priests, all power—political, economic and ecclesiastical—was placed into the hands of a few.

Yes, a world system was formed and, although awesome in retrospect and with the potential for perpetuation of Antichrist's system, was eventually suppressed, but not destroyed. This menacing marauder is only sleeping.

The time was not right for it to come to its full fruition. History still had to come about. Then God did it. Amazing as it may seem, many events came about in rapid succession—again not by chance. The invention of the printing press and the first book produced (the Bible), which brought light to countless thousands living in a darkened world; the use of gunpowder for weaponry; the use of the compass for navigation; the discovery of America; and of course, the great Protestant reformation were all part of God's perfect timing.

Under the able guidance of men like Martin Luther and John Calvin, many began to come out of this system, seeing that man was truly justified by faith apart from works (Ephesians 2:8,9). Various Protestant denominations were formed as they came from the Dark Age world church. Unfortunately in many instances they carried certain practices with them, i.e. baptism of babies, rituals, a priesthood, and various types of representative church governments. Even though the dark ages have ended, it now seems that these so-called Protestant reformation churches are returning home. There is one common bond, expressed by love for mankind, and emphasizing the brotherhood of man and the Fatherhood of God. Various movements are designed to create a bond of unity. The Ecumenical and Charismatic movements along with elements of Neo-Evangelical and liberal modernists (World Council of Churches, National Council of Churches, even the United Nations) are all striving for one thing—unity of purpose and a one-world system.

2
The Demonstration of Present World Conditions

The rule of thumb seems to indicate that the philosophy and compromising attitudes of religious thought in Europe eventually infiltrate the Western Hemisphere twenty to thirty years later. Today, however, it probably takes only five to ten years or even less because of advancements in communication and travel.

The religious community is now reaping the whirlwind of men like Karl Barth, Immanuel Kant, Friedrich Schleiermacher, Soren Kierkegaard, Albrect Ritschl, Adolph Harnack and others. These deep thinkers of liberal theology and existentialist philosophy shaped the minds of young Bible scholars, who eventually taught their same rationale and concepts in Bible schools and colleges around the world. Various types of reasoning on salvation were the predominant factors in their thoughts, sometimes missing Christ entirely. Because of these factors many institutions of higher learning have slipped into the nether world of religion. Such schools as Princeton, Yale, and Harvard were founded upon sound doctrine, but today not so much as a glimmer of fundamental truth can be found in them.

When compromise occurs, it is usually accompanied by a deterioration of moral standards and weakened doctrines. Unless you have been living in total isolation and are oblivious to what has been happening to the moral standards of the world at large, you will readily see this decline. People become conditioned very readily to new standards that even their parents or grandparents would cringe at. At one point even the world's standards and morals were high to a degree. During its inception as a nation, we find that God's word prevailed in the United States and was held in high esteem. The Bible was used in schools and honored by politicians, while at the same time we maintained separation of church and state.

Lately, however, there is unrest with the now generation. Everything is an instant now—even instant religion. The Johnny-come-lately cults seem to pop out of the woodwork every day, expanding at an alarming rate and brainwashing our young people into a Christless eternity. The crime rate is accelerating, and dope, illicit sex, thievery, homosexuality, women's lib, abortion and the breakdown in the family unit are at all time epidemic proportions.

Why do we mention these things? Simply to show, while reviewing present world conditions, that a spiritual vacuum has been created. A void must be filled and people who find no peace or satisfaction and who do not examine the doctrine and teachings of their churches to see if they are based on God's Word are prime candidates for membership into a one-world church.

The subtle phenomenon is creeping in unnoticed. In its embryonic state we find practically every major denomination gathering together for ecumenical services in each other's churches, sharing literature, pulpits and people. When this happens something has to go, be ignored, or compromised, usually the major doctrines of the faith. The one catalyst bringing union is a thing called love.

Everyone wants and needs love. Everyone wants to share fellowship and this seems good. Jesus constantly spoke of the love of God and the brethren. Regardless of our feelings, however, if the systems at work are unbiblical, leave them to themselves. 2 Corinthians 6:14-18 states:

> *"Be ye not unequally yoked together with unbelievers: for what fellowship hath righteousness with unrighteousness? and what communion hath light with darkness? And what concord hath Christ with Belial? Or what part hath he that believeth with an infidel? And what agreement hath the temple of God with idols. For ye are the temple of the living God; as God hath said, I will dwell in them, and walk in them; and I will be their God, and they shall be my people. Wherefore come out from among them, and be ye separate, saith the Lord, and touch not the unclean thing; and I will receive you."*

Those who would deny the Deity of Christ, the Virgin Birth, the vicarious atonement, the death, burial and bodily resurrection of Jesus Christ; who sacrifice Him afresh daily (bloodless or otherwise); who honor Mary as co-redemptrix; who claim a continuing source of extra-Biblical revelation from God apart from His Word; who rely upon visions, signs and wonders; who use Biblical terminology but mean something entirely different; and especially who have never been born again by faith in Jesus Christ—from such withdraw in manners of ecclesiastical and worldly separation.

It must be said at this point that separation is not isolation. We must make every effort to expose the counterfeits and the danger of Antichrist and the formation of his one-world church and also educate true seekers to the glorious Gospel of truth and lead them to the saving knowledge of Christ.

Humanism may make logical deductions by systematically focusing on the positives of world unity: no more wars, strength in numbers, elimination of starvation, international monetary system and standards of measure, and above all else the brotherhood of man and the Fatherhood of God. All these aspects of a one-world system at first glance seem to be noteworthy. There is a problem however. What must be given up in order to achieve this so-called Utopia society? What does God say in His Word? Will a Utopia society ever come about apart from the return of Christ to earth to set up His millennial kingdom? Lastly, what was the outcome of those in Old Testament times who compromised God's directives and had fellowship and intermarriage with the heathen? The answer is readily apparent: in every case destruction and God's vengeance on the rebellious lot given into idolatry.

Dr. Ernest Pickering has compiled a list of seven Biblical imperatives of why those of sound faith should not have any rapport with the works of darkness or those who would bring in another Gospel and doctrine.

> (1) We are to separate from those who are not sound in the faith. "*Having a form of godliness, but denying the power thereof: from such turn away.*" (2 Timothy 3:5)
>
> (2) We are not to assist the cause of the ungodly.
> "*And Jehu the son of Hanani the seer went out to meet him, and said to king Jehoshaphat, Shouldest thou help the ungodly, and love them that hate the Lord? therefore is wrath upon thee from before the Lord.*" (2 Chronicles 19:2)

(3) We are not to give honor to one who denies the faith.

"I marvel that ye are so soon removed from him that called you into the grace of Christ unto another gospel: Which is not another; but there be some that trouble you, and would pervert the gospel of Christ. But though we, or an angel from heaven, preach any other gospel unto you than that which we have preached unto you, let him be accursed." (Galatians 1:6-9)

(4) We are to examine a person's theological position and find it acceptable before cooperating with him in spiritual efforts.

"Beloved, believe not every spirit, but try the spirits whether they are of God: because many false prophets are gone out into the world." (I John 4:1)

(5) We are commanded not to join forces with unbelievers in the Lord's work.

"Be ye not unequally yoked together with unbelievers: for what fellowship hath righteousness with unrighteousness? and what communion hath light with darkness?" (2 Cor. 6:14)

(6) We are not to emphasize unity at the expense of doctrinal purity.

". . . ye should earnestly contend for the faith which was once delivered unto the saints." (Jude 3)

(7) We are not to encourage or cooperate with persons of unsound doctrine.

"If there come any unto you, and bring not this doctrine, receive him not into your house, neither bid him God speed: For

> *he that biddeth him God speed is partaker of his evil deeds.*" (2 John 10,11)[1]

There is one thing for sure on the horizon of apostasy. Religious institutions and organizations are undermining what God emphatically declares in matters of separation. In the following chapters an attempt will be made to expose the intentions and goals of those who may try to persuade folks to leave a solid foundation and venture forth upon the sinking sands of compromise and untruth. Those who are creating waves of dissension are shaking the sleeping giant, the one-world church, who is now beginning to stir.

3

The Demands of Ecumenism

A definition of ecumenism would be good at the outset of this chapter. The word itself has its roots in the Greek "oikoumene"—meaning the inhabited world. The thought of spreading the Gospel to the inhabited world would indeed seem Biblical, especially in fulfilling the great commission, Matthew 28:19-20. The true Christian should have an earnest desire to be ecumenical in the strictest sense of the word, even though the adjective and the noun are not used in the Bible in any special way.

It is unfortunate that certain idioms have a way of taking on new meanings from that which was originally intended. The Pictorial Bible Dictionary makes a statement on this timely topic:

> *"...the efforts of the churches to work together and to try to achieve closer unity have been commonly styled the Ecumenical Movement... Yet there are aspects of contemporary ecumenicism which demand care and caution. In some quarters there is the tendency to think of it more strictly in ecclesiastical terms. This may find expression in the unbiblical and*

> *undesirable hope of ultimately constructing a single world-church under central control... Moreover, there is the danger of the desire for ecumenicity taking precedence of Christian confession in the strict sense... Fortunately, the World Council has thus far clung to a minimal confession of Jesus Christ as Savior and God, but many local supporters would prefer to weaken this in order to include, e.g., Unitarians.'*[2]

That is it in a nutshell. Upon closer scrutiny, four disturbing facts come to focus: (1) A single World Church under central control, (2) Ecumenicity taking precedence over Christian confession, (3) World Council clinging to a minimal confession of Jesus Christ as Savior and God, (4) A weakening of doctrine to include Unitarians.

Any one of the above areas would be grounds enough to withdraw from and separate oneself in matters of diluting God's Word so that it is no longer the Gospel of truth. God never intended for His Word to be watered down and never made provisions for any such compromise. The eternal Word of God may prick the heart of the hearer, bring conviction, lead to salvation, and above all else will not return void (Isaiah 55:11).

We would not in any way degrade people or withdraw from them, but only withdraw from the movements in which they are caught up. Things change slowly and people become conditioned and adapt to new ideals and thought. This can be seen upon the screens of television sets across the land. When a family sits down together to watch a baseball or football game they are bombarded with beer commercials, previews of immoral movies, and semi-nude cheerleaders. Ten to twenty years ago the F.C.C. would have put the station off the air. When it creeps in slowly, that is when the danger is the greatest. P.O.W.'s coming back from Vietnam often commented on the laxity of the moral standards that had taken place during their incarceration. It is when the exposure comes day by day, little by little, that Christians should be exceptionally conscious of the Devil's plan of deception.

Those who have no Biblical foundation for their faith could, over a period of years, be far removed from the beliefs of their ancestors.

On a recent church survey one lady declared: "Oh! Preachers come and go. I have seen my share of them over the past forty years; they all have something different to offer. As long as I go to church, give my money, sing in the choir and attend the social functions, I am satisfied and what will be will be."

Well, that is what is wrong. Too many people are saying what will be will be. Soon central control will dictate to churches what to preach and teach and what materials to use, completely removing the autonomy of every local church. When this happens in its fullest form, then the man of sin himself will demand total allegiance, receiving worship as the very God. The spirit of Antichrist is working now, molding and manipulating people. It can not be clearer than that. Read what God has to tell us about this man of sin. *"Who opposeth and exalteth himself above all that is called God, or that is worshipped; so that he as God sitteth in the temple of God, shewing himself that he is God. For the mystery of iniquity doth already work; only he who now letteth will let, until he be taken out of the way."* (2 Thessalonians 2:4 & 7)

Know this: transition takes time. On the horizon and coming closer lurks one preparing for battle. His battlements are sure. His ranks are forming and gaining momentum. When the time is ripe and God withdraws His restraints, then shall the man of sin take central control and total domination of the one-world church.

It certainly would appear that Ecumenism is one way that Satan chooses to gather together peoples into His camp. Included are those without solid foundations, those who have a form of godliness but deny the power thereof (2 Timothy 3:5), those with minimal confession of Christ as Saviour, those who have watered down the Gospel to make it more palatable to many who might not otherwise join their forces, and finally, those who do not know and do not care if they know what is going on.

4

The Deception of Charismatic Workers

Most individuals are attracted to the unknown. Curiosity and inquisitive attitudes find no age barrier. For millenniums magical tricks and the sleight of hand have astonished folks young and old with Oh's and Ah's. Tricks are a matter of deception and even in the spiritual realm miraculous occurrences can be and are deceptive.

We find Pharaoh's sorcerers imitating the miracles of God. Simon the sorcerer even tried to buy the power of the Holy Spirit in Acts 8:13-19, and miracle men of today are leading gullible people into religions based upon sight, not faith.

It must be said at this point before we proceed any further that it is not the intention of this writer to prove that miracles, signs and extra-Biblical revelations are not for today. It might be said, however, that if these things are for today, our Bibles would instantly become outdated books and anything would go. Who would know what to believe or who to believe? Anyone who claimed some sort of miraculous manifestation could start a new religious cult. This has already been done on numerous occasions. Mormons and Seventh Day Adventists are excellent examples.

Our rulebook, the inerrant, inspired Word of God, gives us glimpses into the future. In so doing, it paints a vivid portrait of how many will be snared into a demonic trap. This will bring unbiblical unity of the masses of humanity, culminating eventually along with ecumenism and other subtle facets of a one-world church.

Someone said: "Well I saw it with my own eyes, I heard it with my own ears, it must be from God." Usually this is the pattern. Someday you or someone you know will grow old or sick. At such times depression and remorse will set in amid a searching heart trying to find an answer. We would pray to God at times such as these for healing and that His perfect will be done. Some dare to say that God wants everybody to be healed and well, and if no healing comes that one does not have enough faith. How cruel this is. Some of the dearest friends I have known have gone to heaven after many months or years of pain and sickness. If everyone were to be healed, then no one would go to heaven. Death is God's method of calling His people home. Mary died, as did Joseph, the apostles and great saints of old. They had faith. Psalm 116:15 says: *"Precious in the sight of the Lord is the death of his saints."* The answer is that God's grace is sufficient (2 Corinthians 12:9-10).

2 Timothy 4:3-4 tells us that "*. . . the time will come when they will not endure sound doctrine; but after their own lust shall heap to themselves teachers, having itching ears; and they shall turn away their ears from the truth and shall be turned to fables.*"

I believe that day has arrived. Neo-Pentecostal and various Charismatic groups have crossed denominational lines. They care not about another's doctrine as long as the common bond of experience exists. If a Mormon, Roman Catholic or even a Muslim claims to have spoken in tongues, they will be received wholeheartedly. It makes no difference if one believes in the deity of Jesus Christ or not, just so the experience occurred that is sufficient. The danger is quite apparent. If compromise is the keynote factor of ecumenism, it is even more so in charismatic circles.

Many who once adhered to true fundamental Biblical doctrines and practices are suddenly falling by the wayward paths. One lady said: "Your church is too strict. You do not permit dancing and 'David danced in the streets.' You do not permit going to the movies, when so many Walt Disney movies are there. You do not permit drinking wine, when wine is mentioned in the Bible so often." It goes on and on, one excuse after another—tobacco, manner of dress, Bingo, social functions—until there is a severance of ties and a regrouping with those who do these things. The Holy Spirit of God brings conviction for holy living. Too many want their cake and want to eat it too. The Word of God spells out very graphically and precisely what mannerisms a child of God should have. We are in the world but not of the world. *"Old things pass away, and all things become new."* (2 Corinthians 5:17) The question one should ask in every situation is: "Is it honoring God?"

I John 2:19 tells us: *"They went out from us, but were not of us"* while I John 2:15 relates *"Love not the world, neither the things that are in the world. If any man love the world the love of the Father is not in him."*

John Benson, author of "Who is the Antichrist?" states *"They were people who at one time had associated with the Christian assembly but who eventually disassociated themselves from it. Their departure from the Christian faith was a manifest evidence that they had never been true Christians at all. For a time they had attended congregational meetings and outwardly assented to apostolic doctrine, but then they finally exhibited what counterfeits they really were. They abandoned the Christian ranks and embraced heretical views."*[8]

Surely if one looks for a church to meet the desire of their heart, evil or good, they can find one. They say that there are homosexual churches for those desiring such, etc. The whole question must be faced honestly and spiritually. Of course a man dead in sins can only play church, not possess it.

The Apostle Paul issued a warning in the day in which he lived. Elements of what we are discussing in this section were prevalent then. They came by other names, but with the same message. Remember, history repeats itself. In Paul's day this spirit of Antichrist was working. As we approach the end times how much more alert we need to be.

May we hold fast the faithful Word of God and not be taken in by false prophets, no matter how sincere they may appear. Ephesians 4:14 relates to this fact. *"That we henceforth be no more children, tossed to and fro, and carried about with every wind of doctrine, by the sleight of men, and cunning craftiness, whereby they lie await to deceive…"* While Matthew 24:24 tells us *"For there shall arise false Christs, and false prophets, and shall shew great signs and wonders; insomuch that, if it were possible, they shall deceive the very elect."*

Many folks I am sure are earnest in desire and are truly saved by the blood of Jesus. But regardless of this fact, they are being used unknowingly as puppets on a string in the formation of a world church that seems so good to them.

Miracles of today are not of God but of Satan. A distinguishing mark of a miracle of God is that it is always either revelatory or redemptive. In light of this and with the Word of God complete in the Bible, we are admonished not to add or subtract from the Holy Word—Deuteronomy 4:2; Revelation 22:18, 19. Redemption is an accomplished fact based upon Calvary's cross and those who receive Him and His finished work. If there were a miracle today it would be the miracle of the new birth. The unexplained seemingly miraculous phenomena of today are not of God but of Satan. He and his cohorts are the modern miracle workers. In the not too far distant future miracles of Satan will abound as common place. They will be accepted with open arms by many. This development seems to be upon us now in its embryonic form. Revelation 16:17 says "*...for they are the spirits of devils, working miracles, which go forth unto the kings of the earth and the whole world.*"

People will have to become conditioned to receive miracle men. It will not happen overnight. The wheels are in motion and the gears have been grinding and have been for centuries. Roman Catholics, for instance, have always been a charismatic people. Visions of Mary and the saints have had a profound influence upon countless millions whom pray and worship all but God. A requirement for beatification to sainthood is that a miracle be attributed to the canonized saint. Countless grottos and shrines have been erected, many times on the exact site where the supposed vision or miracle took place. These so-called holy places are well stocked with empty wheelchairs and crutches, attesting to the fact that something really did happen. The credit is given to the Virgin Mary and saints and rarely to God. Loraine Boettner in his book on Roman Catholicism says: "*Almost every religious order dedicates itself to the Virgin Mary. National shrines, such as those at Lourdes in France, Fatima in Portugal, and Our Lady of Guadalupe in Mexico, are dedicated to her and attract millions.... Thousands of churches, schools, hospitals, convents and shrines are dedicated to her glory.*" "*It is difficult for Protestant denominations to realize the deep love and reverence that devout Roman Catholics have for the Virgin Mary. One must be immersed in and saturated with the Roman Catholic mind in order to feel its heart beat.*"[4]

Many modern Protestant denominations are riding the

pendulum of charismania believing like Catholics, that they must work something up in a spiritual ecstasy.

The father of lies, the author of confusion, is accomplishing his task. His ministers are now at work in churches, behind pulpits, in classrooms, on radio and television and through literature. Sincere searching people are the victims who are taken unawares.

God has not left his elect empty-handed. Warning after warning is given in His Word. I am astounded that men cannot see the light if they claim to be truly saved. Pay heed to the admonition found in 2 Corinthians 11:13-15: *"For such are false apostles, deceitful workers, transforming themselves into the apostles of Christ. And no marvel; for Satan himself is transformed into an angel of light. Therefore it is no great thing if his ministers also be transformed as the ministers of righteousness; whose end shall be according to their works."*

It was mentioned earlier that that day is upon us, perhaps in its embryonic state. It is building and gaining nourishment until when it finally hatches it will unleash havoc and misery throughout the world.

I am always amazed to see people come and go to church without a Bible. I visited a church one Sunday at the request of a friend and carried my Bible as usual. Everyone thought I was a guest speaker. Preachers stand in pulpits and tell stories, tickle people's ears, preach a social gospel, maybe have some sort of a healing ceremony and the people go away starved spiritually. I have been to churches and tent meetings where folks young and old were swaying back and forth with arms raised, eyes closed as if in some kind of hypnotic trance, making strange incoherent gibberish sounds. It reminded me of the pagan tribes found on some South Pacific Islands. It is any wonder they follow workers of religious quackery like Jim Jones?

When a man arrives in town and a church advertises he has

come to heal the common cold or the sniffles and people turn out by the numbers, it frightens me. When a newspaper advertises that a young girl is going to be in church Sunday speaking in tongues, it frightens me. When alabaster vials of holy water and oil are sold for healing of sore bodies, it frightens me. What is going to happen to the multitudes who cry out to a counterfeit God in vain? I believe Matthew 7:21-23 will supply us with the answer: *"Not everyone that saith unto me, Lord, Lord, shall enter into the kingdom of heaven; but he that doeth the will of my Father which is in heaven. Many will say to me in that day. Lord, Lord, have we not prophesied in thy name? and in thy name have cast out devils? and in thy name done many wonderful works? And then will I profess unto them, I never knew you: depart from me, ye that work iniquity."*

People must wake up, lest they are caught off guard and are included with the group mentioned in the aforesaid verse.

It may be that you have a tendency to be skeptical up to this point. Evidence is not the necessary ingredient of this work, however it is this writer's hope that seeds are being planted and that they will take root into a strong belief and faith in serving Jesus Christ based on sure Biblical doctrines. The word doctrine is found forty-four times in the New Testament. In many of these references Christians are admonished to be grounded in sound doctrine and shun false doctrine. Somebody once said to me: *"I have had enough doctrine and rules. All through my life I have been confronted with a series of rules. I was in the green berets and all they had was strict rules and regulations. I do not want any more. I have finally found a church where anyone can do their own thing based on their feelings and experience with Jesus Christ."* We can never make any apologies for the Word of God. To refuse God's way is to be rebellious indeed. If God tells us how to worship Him, pray, fellowship, serve and live for Him we had better do it, for surely we will be held accountable.

Men will come preaching another Gospel. When they come it

is my hope that you may be a discerner and search the Scriptures as the Bereans of old, to see if these things really are so, Acts 17:11.

There is more to come. Continue to read with an open heart and mind, asking the Holy Spirit to be your teacher.

5

The Difference Between the True and Counterfeit Church

For every truth of God the Devil has a counterfeit. Religion is and has been his biggest means of deception through the ages. Basically there are just two religions in the world, if indeed they could be called religions. The two are: works and grace. The biggest obstacle facing the unsaved man is the fact that he can do nothing to procure his salvation. Salvation is totally and completely from the Lord. Humanistic logic, however, dictates another view. Inherent in man is the fact that he wants some of the credit. This is the basis of humanism. It is not so much a premise as it is a fact. But, for the true children of God all praise and honor and glory will be toward the King of Glory, the Lord Jesus Christ, forever.

The unsaved group finds itself dead in sin and followers of the prince of the power of the air, Ephesians 2:1-3. It becomes readily apparent that these folks are the prime candidates in Satan's one-world church. Proverbs 16:25 says *"There is a way which seemeth right unto a man, but the end thereof are the ways of death."* The fact of the matter is that you either do it God's way or not at all!

This bit of introduction into this chapter sets the background for determining if you are in the true church or the counterfeit church. Someone once asked me why there are so many different types of churches.

To answer that question a short review of church history is necessary. Let us look at it from the very beginning, and discover its founder, foundation head, members, doctrine, and duration.

While Jesus was still in His public ministry, just before the crucifixion, He made this amazing statement in Matthew 16:18: *"And I say also unto thee. That thou art Peter, and upon this rock I will build my church, and the gates of hell shall not prevail against it."* This verse has been so abused and misinterpreted that it has probably been the major point in the formation of a papacy and the establishment of apostolic succession. Let us diagnose this verse in its entirety to determine if it has any significance or relevance to these latter days.

At once it becomes apparent that His church is still future when Jesus said "I will build my church." The church, therefore, is not to be found prior to this date, nor is it found in the Old Testament. The word for church is ecclesia which means a called out assembly. Although there were many called out assemblies apart from the assembly of Jesus Christ (i.e. Acts 7:38; 19:32, 39, 41), the assembly or congregation which Jesus spoke of was clearly unique. It is composed of all regenerate members who have been born again by the Spirit of God and baptized into his body. Titus 3:5 tells us that this regeneration is accomplished by the Holy Spirit, not by any works that any might do to procure from God some favorable status. (Acts 10:34 states that God is no respecter of persons, and Ephesians 2:8 says that salvation is the gift of God, not of works, lest any man should boast, or have any room for boasting.)

This distinct group was called Christians, not Catholics, Protestants, or any other group which permeates the globe today—Acts 11:26 *"And the disciples were called Christians first in Antioch."* Today all major denominations and even some cults bear the title of Christian. But do they have the right, Biblically speaking, to use this title? Are they professors or possessors?

Proceeding further we find that this body of believers which forms the true church of Jesus Christ was still future in Acts 1:5: *"For John truly baptized with water; but ye shall be baptized with the Holy Spirit not many days from now."* This verse shows that the Church is still future to the ascension to heaven of Jesus Christ. Acts 2:1-4 records for us the birth of the Church. Note the four strange phenomena mentioned: speaking in unlearned languages (tongues) by the Apostles (the Galilians, vs. 7); tongues as of fire; the sound of a mighty wind; and the filling of the Holy Ghost. As we put together more facts, we inductively can start to draw conclusions. When the first Gentile convert, Cornelius, was added to the body of Christ (Acts 11:15-16) we see that the birth of the Church can now be traced to a point between Acts 1:5 and Acts 11:15-16. It can be none other than Acts: 2, which is the birth of the Church Jesus spoke of back in Matthew 16:18.

Some teach that the body of Christ is composed of two groups of believers—those who have been baptized into the body of Christ and have received certain spiritual gifts (the haves), and those who have not realized this as yet (the have nots). This contradicts the Scriptures in every way as we read 1 Corinthians 12:13: *"For by one Spirit are we all baptized into one body, whether we be Jews or Gentiles, whether we be bond or free; and have been all made to drink into one Spirit."* for you see that "all" were baptized into the Church, not those who exhibited certain sign gifts. Also, it might be brought to the reader's attention that the word for baptize is the Greek word "baptizzo" which means to place into, dip or immerse. Thus it is a good word to indicate the believer's being placed into the body of Christ. At the Last Supper when Jesus dipped the sop, the word used was "baptizzo" and when Jesus returns He will have on a vesture dipped in blood (baptizzo).

Getting back to Matthew 16:18, another very important aspect must be cleared up if one is to derive the real understanding of what is being said. Please follow carefully what this writer is about to say. It may change your whole outlook as to who the head of the Church is. Now watch: Jesus, speaking to the Apostle Peter says, *"Thou art Peter* (Petros, meaning a stone or pebble), *and upon this rock* (Petra, a massive boulder) *I will build my church."*

What does this mean to us? Notice, as I paraphrase what Jesus is saying to Peter: Peter, you are just a little pebble, but upon this massive boulder (pointing to Himself) I will build My Church. You can clearly see the implications of this statement. Jesus is the one on whom the Church is built. Just after this, Jesus again speaks to Peter and actually calls him Satan (Matthew 16:23). Other verses verify the fact that the Church is built on Jesus even more precisely: He is the *"...head over all things to the church"* (Ephesians 1:22); and *"...Jesus Christ Himself being the chief corner stone"* (Ephesians 2:20). In other verses we read that the Church is the bride of Christ (Revelation 22:17); the wife (Revelation 19:7,8); the temple of the Holy Ghost (1 Corinthians 3:16, 6:19); and the body of Christ (Ephesians 5:23-32; Romans 12:4; Colossians 1:18). The "keys to the kingdom of heaven" mentioned in Matthew 16:19 refer to the Gospel message, which all believers can use to show unbelievers the way to heaven. We simply cannot exhaust a study of such magnitude in this limited manuscript. It is, however, our hope that new light has been shed in relation to the Church's beginnings and propagation.

The Church of the apostolic era was for the most part good. It had problems in infancy, which could be corrected by a living apostle. Many of the difficulties encountered by these baby churches were remedied by an exhortation and encouragement in one of the epistles, which of course compose our Bibles today. All Scripture is given by the inspiration of God (God-breathed). Holy men of God wrote as they were moved by the Holy Ghost (2 Timothy 3:16, 2 Peter 1:21). These Scriptures have been preserved intact over the centuries of time, not the original manuscripts, but good and accurate copies of same.

The apostles have gone on to heaven, while the Word of God lives on. Matthew 5:18 says *"Till heaven and earth pass, one jot or one tittle shall in no way pass from the law, till all be fulfilled."* The Bible reveals God's doctrine and sets the pattern for worship and fellowship. It is infallible and inerrant. No man alive or dead can make this claim, although they have tried and are still trying. Galatians 1:7, 8 states; *"...But though we, or an angel from heaven, preach any other gospel unto you than that ye have received, let him be accursed."*

The true Church stands by the Word of God alone. The counterfeit church will stand by the dogmas and inventions of men. The embryonic church will exhibit all the characteristics of apostasy, making it easy for blinded men to follow Antichrist. Jesus Christ said in John 8:32: *"You shall know the truth and the truth shall set you free".*

The answers to the questions posed earlier are now answered. Let us review:

1. The true Church's beginning: Pentecost, Acts 2.

2. The founder: the Rock (Petra), the Lord Jesus Christ, Matthew 16:18.

3. Its foundation: The Apostles, with Jesus Christ the Chief Cornerstone, Ephesians 2:20.

4. Its head: Jesus Christ, the head of the Body, Ephesians 1:22.

5. Its members: All regenerate members from Pentecost to the rapture, Acts 2; 1 Thessalonians 4:13.

6. Its doctrine: The Word of God, 2 Timothy 3:16.

7. Its duration: forever in heaven, John 3:16.

The facts gathered from Matthew 16:18 do indeed show that the Church was established upon Christ Jesus as its head. But what about the apostles? How do they fit in? Did they appoint certain men to take their place after they passed off the scene? It becomes apparent that one must know whether or not they did appoint such men, and if so, what authority they have, what the requirements are for being an apostle, and whether or not there are any today.

I receive literature from time to time from folks who claim that the Apostle of love, the Apostle from the east, the Apostle of health, etc. will be in their churches on a given day conducting services. Is this Scriptural? If it is, then by all means follow and praise God for working in our midst. If it is unscriptural, however, then by all means avoid them, withdraw, and serve the living Savior in truth and in light.

The general meaning of the word "apostle" (apostello) is one called or commissioned for a specific task. In its broadest sense I suppose the term may be used by one who may be a missionary to a particular people and quite appropriately. However, the term apostle seems to conjure up in most people's minds the thought of one chosen by Christ, i.e. the original twelve. In the early church the office of an apostle was unique in that it was a spiritual gift as well as an office. Ephesians 4:11tells us: *"And he gave some, apostles; and some, prophets, and some, evangelists; and some, pastors and teachers."* Certain of these offices have passed off the scene with the passing of the apostolic era and the completion of the Bible, namely apostles and prophets. Let us examine the Word of God to see why.

An apostle was chosen and hand picked by Jesus Christ. No one ever sought the office of an apostle. It was bestowed by the sovereign will of God. That also goes for any spiritual gift. Read the gospels and see how the selection process occurred. Check Matthew 4:19; 9:9; 10:1-5 to see how Jesus chose some. In Acts 9 we read how Saul of Tarsus was chosen, and later became Paul the apostle.

Also along with being hand picked by Jesus, one had to be a witness to the resurrected Christ. 1 Corinthians 9:1,2 speaks of Paul seeing the resurrected Christ and John 20:19-20 speaks of the resurrected Christ appearing to the eleven apostles, and then to Thomas who was absent. John 15:16 and Matthew 28:19, 20 show that the apostles were chosen and sent out by Christ.

We may also add that all of the apostles suffered martyrdom for the sake of Christ and that the working of miracles was indeed a sign of an apostle, Acts 2:43 *"And fear came upon every soul: and many wonders and signs were done by the apostles."* and Hebrews 2:4 *"God also bearing them witness, both with signs and wonders, and with divers miracles, and gifts of the Holy Ghost, according to his own will?"*

In light of the aforesaid information, no one today can dictate God's Word, bring forced interpretations, or claim infallibility or declare that they and they alone have this privilege by the right of apostolic succession. Each man has individual soul liberty, to read and understand God's Word as the Holy Spirit guides. 1 John 2:27 says: *"…and ye need not that any man teach you; but as the same anointing teacheth you of all things, and is truth, and is no lie, and even as it hath taught you, ye shall abide in him,"* while 1 Corinthians 2:13 tells us: *"Which things also we speak, not in the words which man's wisdom teacheth, but which the Holy Spirit teacheth, comparing spiritual things with spiritual."*

This chapter title is "The Difference Between The True and Counterfeit Church." It would be this writer's hope that some light has been shed about those who have come, and are still to come, with great authority from men, claiming to be modern apostles, miracle workers, and the true leaders of Antichrist's counterfeit church in its embryonic form.

6
The Devious Wolves

There are certain men, ministers of Christ, who no doubt mean well, who help their fellowmen, do good in their community and even pray to God. These men have most ignorantly been laying the road on which the world will be traveling to Antichrist and his super church.

Antichrist and the world church go together. His work is intricately bound up in religion as well as politics and economics. You can hardly mention one without the other. He will need his recruits. How will he get them and from where will they come? I am sure that no one will intentionally sign up if they know it is Satan's organization. If this were the case no one would join and nothing would come about. The world church would not form. A church system is only as good as its members and with no followers there is no system.

Satan knows this and he proceeds subtly, deceptively, and patiently, manipulating men's minds and thoughts so that unknowingly and in earnest desire they press forth to paths of destruction. Jude tells us in verse 4: "...*For there are certain men crept in unawares, who were before of old ordained, to this condemnation, ungodly men, turning the grace of our God into lasciviousness, and denying the only Lord God, and our Lord Jesus Christ."*

These certain men have crept in already. They appear as ministers of light, denying the grace of God that brings salvation and declaring a message based upon humanism and sheer speculation of how things should be.

The central message of the Bible is the death, burial, resurrection and soon coming of our Lord and Savior Jesus Christ. The central message is not good works, love for your fellowman, healing the sick, speaking in tongues, feeding the hungry, striving for unity of the masses or a pure truncated social gospel. One could realistically do all these things and go to hell.

Dr. Ernest Pickering writes directly to this topic:

> *"An unscriptural pietism has pervaded Christendom. To these pietists sharp conflicts over doctrine are inconsistent with love. Pietism says, 'the mark of true discipleship is love not doctrine.' Most unfortunately, this type of thinking is exerting considerable influence, not only among liberals (where you would expect to find it), but also among conservatives. Men, who for years have stood staunchly against compromise with liberalism and neo-orthodoxy, are now advocating in the interests of love, a rapprochement with them.*
>
> *"Forgotten is the fact that the New Testament emphasizes sound doctrine as well as love. Sound doctrine must be held in love, but love without sound doctrine is a body without a skeletal structure, a theological jellyfish…*
>
> *"Biblical separatists must never abdicate strong, Scriptural doctrinal position for the purpose of demonstrating love. The strongest love which one can have for God and man*

is that love which is rooted in the entire truth of God, and which will not deviate there from."[5]

The liberals and modernists with their existential philosophies, who teach that sin is only relative and in the mind of the beholder, who support communist regimes and who would compromise God's word to bring their global cause to its conclusion are the wolves in sheep's clothing.

Matthew 7:15 relates to this clearly: *"Beware of false prophets, which come to you in sheep's clothing, but inwardly they are ravening wolves."*

The attitude of modernism is a menacing octopus, which stretches forth its tentacles, trapping and ensnaring and squeezing the very spiritual life from those who are unknowingly caught up in this awful mess. Any tendency to weaken the standards or doctrinal convictions will sink the ship of truth. Unfortunately the ship is now listing badly and some are going down for the last time.

Dr. Mark Jackson in his book "Ready, Set, Grow" ties certain modernist groups together in the same camp when he says: "*The modernists developed an offshoot called, among other names, neo-orthodoxy; the fundamentalists saw a new group arise called neo-evangelicals. The neo-orthodox, with little or no doctrinal convictions and in too many cases very little scruples, (e.g., 'situation ethics,' actual encouragement of pre-marital and extra-marital sex, involvement in civil disobedience, encouragement of minorities to revolt—using force—if necessary, jazz worship services, total fellowship across all doctrinal and denominational lines, including Mohammedanism, Catholicism, Judaism, etc.), and the neo-evangelicals, (with their fundamental orthodoxy and Bible truth but with no convictions about separation from unbelief and who find one of their greatest delights in 'dialoguing' with theneo-orthodox and liberal, while poking fun at their former associates in the fundamentalist ranks), see themselves as bridges for cooperation and possibly, ultimate, amalgamation."*[6]

It is imperative that other organizations be identified who work in conjunction with the aforesaid groups of ecumenism. The World Council of Churches and the National Council of Churches have close rapport with the United Nations and Catholicism. They have one intention—expansion into global affairs. Since its inception in 1948 it has expanded to include over 100 countries and 500 million members. The secular encyclopedia, Funk and Wagnalls, related these facts:

"WORLD COUNCIL OF CHURCHES, international organization of Protestant, Anglican, Old Catholic, and Orthodox churches, founded in 1948 to promote ecumenical fellowship, service, and study…

Major units of the council's organization include the divisions of Ecumenical Action, of Inter Church Aid, Refugee, and World Service, and of World Mission and Evangelism; the commission on Faith and Order; and the Commission of the Churches on International Affairs."[7]

Once again it should be noted that strength and numbers go hand in hand. The World Council and its affiliate the National Council of Churches in the United States are rapidly becoming the representative spokesmen in matters of clerical consultation. The 1980 hostage crisis in Iran saw clergy selected from the World Council of Churches or those with close ties to them, not from any fundamentalist independent groups. When new communities are being constructed, land for churches is allocated for churches associated with the National Council of Churches and not for any fundamental groups, especially those that would hold to a separatist stand.

The forces are at work and soon, very soon, the wolves will shed their sheep's clothing. The bad part, however, is that it will be too late. The whole conglomeration will be blended together into the Antichrist's temporary kingdom. The embryonic satellites would include many groups. Some have been mentioned already, but the list goes on—the ecumenical movement, the charismatic movements, the World Council of Churches, the National Council of Churches, Roman Catholicism, neo-Pentecostals, liberals, modernists, neo-orthodox and neo-evangelical groups. Leaven works slowly but surely, and its spread eventually permeates the whole loaf or lump. Galatians 5:9; 1 Corinthians 5:6, 7.

From its birth the early church grew exponentially and in no time at all became a spiritual power that even the Roman Empire could not contend with. The problem of today is that the churches are only growing by addition. The swing of the tide is now toward compromise and not toward the faith which was once delivered to the saints (Jude 3). Unless the fire of indifference is quenched, we may be the generation of people who will see the undermining of the true faith of Jesus Christ.

May we who are faithful endurers see and know for a surety that *"the gates of hell will not prevail against it (the church)"* and although *heaven and earth will pass away God's Word will never pass away."* Matthew 16:18 & 24:35.

7
The Doomed Have Been Warned

Before making any attempt to identify the world church of which the embryonic satellites are a part, the warning has to be issued.

By no means has this author attempted to set any dates for the eventual religious takeover of society, the return of Christ, the tribulation, or any areas of God's eschatological program. All we are saying is that we had better become aware of the world around us and look heaven bound even as the apostle. He issued warning after warning. He saw the bloody massacre of the Christians under Nero's savage tyranny. As Paul wrote under the inspiration of the Holy Spirit, he no doubt was well aware of each facet of Antichrist's domain but not of the timing, thinking that it would happen in his lifetime. In certain key passages of scriptures he included himself with those who will be caught up at the rapture of the Body of Christ. The use of the pronoun "we" confirms this fact, e.g., 1 Thessalonians 4:14-17. *"For if we believe that Jesus died and rose again, even so them also which sleep in Jesus will God bring with him. For this we say unto you by the word of the Lord, that we which are alive and remain unto the coming of the Lord shall not prevent them which are asleep. For the Lord himself shall descend from heaven with a shout, with the voice of the archangel, and with the trump of God: and the dead in Christ shall rise first: Then we which are alive and remain shall be caught up together with them in the clouds, to meet the Lord in the air: and so shall we ever be with the Lord."*

Later on as the centuries of time rolled by, the early church fathers experienced the same thing as pre-millennialists, believing they would be a part of the last time events. This is called the doctrine of immanency, although a-millennialism, and post-millennialism later became prominent. Generation after generation have been warned. We stand maybe at the consummation of this age.

Never before has mankind had the potential to annihilate itself. Advances in science abound every day. The miracle of electronics makes global communications a normal occurrence. Why, a man can hit a baseball in California and a million viewers can see him hit it at the very same instant in New York. The world is shrinking and the matter of identity of the masses is no longer a problem. I read somewhere that the names of everybody in the United States can fit into a little block no bigger than an ice cube. It used to be that a satellite could take a picture of a golf course from thousands of miles in space, then with some advances in technology it had the ability to take a picture of a green of the golf course, while today they say they can take a picture of the golf ball, and tomorrow the writing on the golf ball.

The book of Daniel, chapter 12, verse 4, written over 2,700 years ago, reveals a major point that we may ponder over: *"But thou, 0 Daniel, shut up the words, and seal the book, even to the time of the end: many shall run to and fro, and knowledge shall be increased."* One has to be blind not to see that this prophecy is literally being fulfilled in our lifetime. People are scurrying about like never before. The highways are congested with bumper to bumper traffic, the jet setters find it no problem at all to skip across continents that would have required their grandparents weeks or even months to accomplish. Before the turn of the century the average man never ventured more than fifty miles from his place of birth, and then it was on horseback. Today men go to the moon in a matter of days. Yes, people are running to and fro. The other point of Daniel's prophecy is that knowledge will be increased. Surely we have already seen this in action. But what about spiritual knowledge being poured out? It was not so many years ago that men would rarely preach on books such as Revelation, Daniel and Ezekiel and when they did they were compelled to spiritualize most of the book away. Today a favorite pulpit topic is eschatology and these great prophetic books.

The only real authority rests with the word of God. It is definite that certain events will come to their culmination. If God wants this generation to be the one that will witness the fulfillment of prophetical eschatological statements, it will be so and will not be thwarted. Even though hundreds and thousands of truth bearers raise their banners high, the inevitable will come to pass.

This book is not intended to delay the inevitable pre-planned program of God but to warn if possible the faithful remnant of God's impending judgment so they may hold fast the faithful word of God and be the over comers in the great day of God's wrath against the harlot, Antichrist and Satan.

Those presently in Christ, who have been sealed by the Holy Spirit, will not be a part of the condemnation. If this book can be influential to any who may be headed into days of tribulation, we would prayerfully say, "Heed the warning" and come out from among the system of whoredom.

Two thousand years ago Jesus warned of deception, global conflict and world sorrows. May Matthew 24:3-13 be quoted and examined to see the cruciality of the time: *"Tell us, when shall these things be? and what shall be the sign of thy coming, and of the end of the age? And Jesus answered and said unto them. Take heed that no man deceives you. For many shall come in my name, saying, I am Christ; and shall deceive many. And ye shall hear of wars and rumours of wars: see that ye be not troubled: for all these things must come to pass, but the end is not yet. For nation shall rise against nation, and kingdom against kingdom: and there shall be famines, and pestilences, and earth quakes, in divers places. All these are the beginning of sorrows...And many false prophets shall rise, and shall deceive many."*

This writer believes that the above warnings can make headline news today in any major newspaper in the world. Someone might say, *"But we have always had these things. What makes you think we are that generation?"* We cannot be dogmatic on this issue and we make no attempt to be. No one can answer that question for sure. The end of this age may be delayed another thousand years. One cannot, however, ignore the world around him.

Before commenting on the passage in Matthew, an important concept should be interjected. God operates on a time calendar different from ours. He can survey the whole panorama of time instantly as a present now. From this omniscient vantage point every perfect detail is before him. An interesting thought comes to the forefront in seeing God incorporate his time system with man's. 2 Peter 3:8 tells us: *"But, beloved be not ignorant of this one thing, that one day is with the Lord as a thousand years, and a thousand years as one day."*

With this time sequence in mind, it must be remembered that God created the world and all that is therein in six days and rested on the seventh. Along with this, as one ponders the theological implications contained in 2 Peter 3:8 he might remember that two thousand years after creation came the call of Abraham; two thousand years after that came the birth of Jesus Christ; and today we are in the final hours of the completion of another two thousand year cycle.

If God is immutable and with no variableness (James 1:17), some sense may be ascertained from this. The prospects are awesome. The Jews operate on a calendar different from ours, using a 360 day year. From the time our modern system of counting time became the accepted method, we have picked up many years, which in reality puts us drastically closer to the end of another 2,000 years of time, plus or minus.

Going back now to Matthew 24:3-13, surely these things mentioned by our Lord Jesus Christ have always abounded but never in such massive proportions or magnitude. Look at the events that will ultimately occur. Every one of these warnings are upon us at this writing and undeniably so:

WARS AND RUMORS OF WARS: why, every month it seems a new skirmish breaks out. Hostility from Asia to Latin America exists, including in Iran, Iraq, Afghanistan, South Africa, Ireland, Poland, El Salvador, and Peru.

FAMINES: why, half the world does not know what it means to have a full stomach. Famine and starvation are prevalent in India, Pakistan, Angola, Cambodia, Vietnam, and even in some sections of inner city and rural America. We find folks with severe malnutrition. It is estimated that over 27,000 people starve to death daily.

EARTHQUAKES: why, the intensity of earthquakes are increasing on a global scale. Scientists say that there is tremendous strain being exerted on our continental plates grinding and churning just waiting for the appropriate moment to release a fury. Do not be surprised if you wake up some morning to hear that a major earthquake has shaken some vastly populated metropolitan city. Review the devastation at Mt. St. Helens, Naples, Nicaragua, and Mexico, all of them shaken by earthquakes.

PESTILENCE: why, who can forget Love Canal, Three Mile Island, the ozone layer, the crop failures due to drought and insects, and the pollution of our land, air, rivers and oceans.

FALSE PROPHETS: why, today they are in almost every town, large and small. They are seen on prime time TV. and heard on radio, in churches, tent meetings, on street corners and in theaters. Of course their modus operandi is miracles, healing and speaking in tongues.

Look around. It is beyond me how a man or a woman can give a testimony at a crusade on national TV. of a miraculous happening in their life, sing a beautiful hymn of the faith to a packed stadium of people, bringing folks to a state of emotional tears, then that night perform in some smoke-filled, booze-infested nightclub, jazzing around a stage to the world's standards. You cannot have Christ and Belial at the same time.

This chapter heading is "The Doomed Have Been Warned." Folks, believe it. Those in Christ will never see Antichrist or his world system in its fullest degree. This author believes in a pre-tribulation rapture of the Body of Christ (the church). Although present day saints will not see the Super Satanic Church in its ultimate stage of development, they will see this false theological giant in its embryonic form. Things will move rapidly after the salt

(Matthew 5:15) (which is a preservative) is taken off the earth, by the removal of the church. The groundwork is being prepared now. The stage is being set and the warning is to the Christian not to be taken in and become the gullible victims of a religious system led by deceived leaders. *"Come out from among them…be ye separate saith the Lord…and I will receive you."* 2 Corinthians 6:17.

8
The Deceitful World Church's Identity

Dare we venture forth so boldly as to claim to know the identity of the World Church or by what name she comes? Certainly her Biblical names are known: *"Mystery Babylon is her name,"* (Revelation 16:19). *"The whore is her name,"* (Revelation 17:1). Also her location is known: *"The seven heads are seven mountains, on which the woman sitteth,"* (Revelation 17:9). Some here have immediately leaped upon Rome herself as the place of central headquarters—the city built on seven hills.

It is an ecclesiastical system, that is for sure. She is *"drunk with the blood of the saints,...and the martyrs of Jesus,"* (Revelation 17:65). *"...The voice of the bridegroom and of the bride shall be heard no more at all in thee,"* (Revelation 18:23). It is a system of pomp and splendor: *"And the woman was arrayed in purple and scarlet colour, and decked with gold and precious stones and pearls, having a golden cup in her hand full of abominations and filthiness of her fornication,"* (Revelation 17:4), and an idolatrous system. The extent of her jurisdiction is the whole earth: *"The waters which thou sawest, where the whore sitteth, are peoples, and multitudes, and nations, and tongues,"* (Revelation 17:15) and *"And the woman which thou sawest is that great city, which reigneth over the kings of the earth"* (Revelation 17:18). She is economic: *"and the merchants of the earth shall weep and mourn over her; for no man buyeth their merchandise any more"* (Revelation 18:11).

C.I. Scofield, in his footnote, concurs with these findings:

> *"The name 'Babylon', in prophecy, is sometimes used in a larger sense than mere reference to either the ancient city or nation. There are two forms which Babylon is to have in the end-time: political Babylon (Revelation 17:8-17) and ecclesiastical Babylon(Revelation 17:1-7, 18; 18:1-24). Political Babylon is the beast's confederated empire, the last form of Gentile world dominion. Ecclesiastical Babylon is all apostate Christendom, in which the Papacy will undoubtedly be prominent; it may very well be that this union will embrace all the religions of the world."* [8]

Now let us put together all the facts in hopes of ascertaining the true identity of the harlot world church:

1. Her names: Mystery Babylon, the Whore
2. Her location: Upon seven hills
3. Her extent: The whole world "upon many waters"
4. She is a system of pomp and splendor, "arrayed in purple and scarlet colour"
5. She is an idolatrous system, "Full of abominations"
6. She is political, "kings of earth"
7. She is economic, "merchants of the earth mourn"
8. She is religious, "drunk with the blood of the martyrs"

In an earlier chapter it was brought out that the world church of the dark ages exhibited all of these features and was either a type of that which is to come, or is that which is yet to come. If the latter be true, she is only sleeping, waiting to be roused. The non-Italian Pope, a world traveler, from a communist country, whose central theme is love and unity of mankind, makes even the most skeptical raise their eyebrows in wonder.

"The Gospel Truth," a monthly publication released by The Southwest Radio Church, relates extraordinary facts in its October, 1978, issue:

The Coming World Church

"The fact that a religious movement is going to affect coming world events is beyond question. According to Malachi Martin in The Last Conclave, The Catholic hierarchy is looking beyond Communism to the bringing in of God's Kingdom on earth in the not distant future. Catholic doctrine stresses that the Kingdom will be brought in through the Church...

"In view of the fact that Malachi Martin, a recognized authority on Vatican affairs, has predicted the 82nd Conclave would be the last, an article in a May 30, 1978 edition of Roses, an ultra-conservative and traditionalist Catholic publication, claims the following revelations from Mary and the Lord Jesus: 'The Church of My Son, that is being stripped of all holiness, shall emerge with the world and the world's leaders, to be directed for a short time by Satan. I have asked you, My children, to pray for your Holy Father, Pope Paul, in Rome... Already those in command, who have assumed command by fraud, are planning his successor, and he shall be the agent of hell. Do not go about despairing your Holy Father, Pope Paul VI. He is not the antichrist. You are deluded in your reasoning if you place this title upon him. He is not the antichrist Pope. The next one shall be he."[9]

The fact that even Roman Catholicism makes this statement should cause all within her grip to re-evaluate their thinking on this vital matter.

As the information is assimilated, the bits and pieces begin to add up and fall into place. In light of what the Rome of today is, in relationship to her Biblical description, some may be disturbed about her economic status. Rome has never been a major importing or exporting city. Her wealth has been gathered by plunder, gifts, and various types of payments for religious activities. Shipping is nil in comparison to New York, Hong Kong, Singapore, Amsterdam, London and so many other cities.

This, however, presents no problem whatsoever. If identity is the vital issue at hand in this chapter, it becomes imperative that one crucial aspect of Rome be brought into focus.

Based upon historical facts and Biblical prophetic fulfillment it can be determined that Rome had an overall world dominance in her heyday, encompassing the European nations from Spain to England, including the Germanic, French, Greek and Turkish nations of today.

The book of Daniel shows very graphically who the ruling power will be in the last days. While interpreting a dream of King Nebuchadnezzar of ancient Babylon, Daniel declares under the inspiration of the Holy Spirit the four leading powers of all time. Daniel 2:31 tells us: *"Thou, O king, sawest, and behold a great image. This great image, whose brightness was excellent, stood before thee; and the form thereof was terrible. This image's head was of fine gold, his breast and his arms of silver, his belly and his thighs of brass, his legs of iron, his feet part of iron and part of clay. Thou sawest till that a stone was cut out without hands, which smote the image upon his feet that were of iron and clay, and brake them to pieces."*

Daniel continues in the following verses of chapter 2 to show that Babylon was the head of gold and ruler *"wheresoever the children of man dwell"*, (verse 38). The key for unlocking the secrets of history past and future is found in the following verses of Daniel *"And after thee shall arise another kingdom inferior to thee, and another third kingdom of brass, which shall bear rule over all the earth. And the fourth kingdom shall be strong as iron: forasmuch as iron breaketh in pieces and subdueth all things: and as iron that breaketh all these, shall it break in pieces and bruise. And whereas thou sawest the feet and toes, part of potters' clay, and part of iron, the kingdom shall be divided; but there shall be in it of the strength of the iron, forasmuch as thou sawest the iron mixed with miry clay."*

In a later vision the ruling powers of the world are declared by name. Daniel 8:20-24 reveals they go by the names Babylon, Media and Persia, Greece, and finally the last and most ferocious one which history acknowledges as none other than mighty Rome. A nation who shall be mighty and destroy the holy people, who cause deceit to prosper and stand against the prince of princes.

The ten toes of Daniel 2:41 and the ten horns of Revelation 13:1 are synonymous. They indicate that the Roman Empire will have ten satellite nations under her jurisdiction, sort of a renewal of the old Roman Empire. Many Bible scholars claim the ten nation Common Market will be part of the beast's world system still in its infancy.

A point to ponder would be that the Imperial Roman Empire under the Caesars was never defeated but deteriorated from within and eventually made a smooth transition to the Holy Roman Empire. Thus she still exists although still in the process of change. The Roman Catholic Church has time after time asserted that she never changes. The fact of the matter is that she has done nothing but change throughout the past two thousand years. If the Lord Jesus Christ returned today He certainly would not recognize Rome as the church He instituted. The mystery of iniquity has been at work subtly, conditioning folks unknowingly so they are ripe to accept Antichrist's charge when he does come.

The following changes and inventions of man have infiltrated

"Holy Mother church" over the centuries and for information purposes it would do well to list them. The early New Testament church of the apostles' day knew nothing of these things which have become accepted practices throughout Catholicism and which are all based on sheer speculation, invention, and doctrines of men and not God. At the Reformation in the 16th century these heresies were repudiated as having no part in the religion of Jesus as taught in the New Testament.

These dates are in many cases approximate and many of these heresies had been practiced in the church years before, but only when they were officially adopted by a church council and proclaimed by the Pope as dogma of faith, did they become binding on Roman Catholics.

1. Prayers for the dead and the sign of the cross—310 AD
2. Wax candles introduced in church—320 AD
3. Tampering with Law of God (Ex. 20:3, 17)—321 AD
4. Veneration of angels and dead saints—375 AD
5. The Mass (unbloody repeat of Calvary's sacrifice) 394 AD
6. The worship of Mary, the use of the term Mother of God (from the Council of Ephesus)—431 AD
7. Priests began to dress different from laity—500 AD
8. The doctrine of purgatory established by Gregory the Great—593 AD
9. The Latin language, as the language of prayer and worship in churches, also by Gregory (the Word of God forbids teaching in an unknown tongue. II Tim. 2:16, I Tim. 6:20.)—600 AD
10. Prayers to Mary and dead saints (strictly forbidden in Bible.) (Matt. 11:23, Lk. 1:46, Acts 10:25-26, 14:14-18)—600 AD
11. The Papacy is of pagan origin. The title of Pope or

universal Bishop was first given to the Bishop of Rome by the wicked Emperor Phocas—610 AD

12. The kissing of the Pope's feet—709 AD

13. Worship of the cross, images and relics—788 AD

14. Holy Water, mixed with a pinch of salt and blessed by a Priest—850 AD

15. Veneration of St. Joseph began—890 AD

16. Canonization of dead saints by Pope John XIV—965 AD

17. Fasting on Friday and during Lent—998 AD

18. Celibacy of the priesthood—1079 AD

19. The Rosary, or prayer beads, by Peter the Hermit, copied from Hindus & Mohammedans—1090 AD

20. The inquisition of heretics by Council of Verona (Jesus never taught the use of force to spread His religion)—1184 AD

21. The sale of indulgences, a purchase of forgiveness by money and prayer for living and dead—1190 AD

22. The dogma of transubstantiation by Pope Innocent III—1215 AD

23. Confession of sins to the priest at least once a year by Pope Innocent III in the Lateran Council (The Gospel commands us to confess our sins directly to God, Ps. 51:1-10; Luke 7:48 I John 1:8-9)—1215 AD

24. The adoration of the wafer (host) decreed by Pope Honorius—1220 AD

25. The Bible forbidden to laymen & placed in the index of forbidden books, Council of Valencia—1229 AD

26. The scapular was invented by Simon Stock, an English monk. It is a piece of brown cloth with the picture of the Virgin Mary and supposed to contain supernatural virtue to protect from all dangers those who wear it on the naked skin—1229 AD

27. The Roman Church forbade cup to the laity—1414 AD

28. The doctrine of purgatory proclaimed as a dogma of faith by Council of Florence—1439 AD
29. The doctrine of 7 Sacraments affirmed—1439 AD
30. The Ave Maria—1503 AD
31. Tradition is of equal authority to Bible—1545 AD
32. The Apocryphal Books added to the Bible—1546 AD
33. The Immaculate Conception of the Virgin Mary—1854 AD
34. Papal Infallibility (dogma proclaimed by Pope Pius IX)—1870 AD

(This is a blasphemy and the sign of the apostasy and of the antichrist predicted by St. Paul, 2 Thess. 2:2-12; Rev. 17:1-9; 13:5-8, 18. Many Bible students see the number of the beast (Rev. 13:18) 666 in the Roman letters of the Pope's title:

"VICARIVS FILII DEI." (V=5, I=1, C=100, I=1, V=5, I=1, L=50, I=1, I=1, D=500, I=1 = 666)

35. All modern discoveries of science condemned if not approved by the Church (Pope Pius X)—1907 AD
36. Public schools condemned (Pius XI)—1930 AD
37. Doctrine that Mary is the "Mother of God", (Pope Pius XI)—1931 AD
38. The Assumption of the Virgin Mary, (Pope Pius XII)—1950 AD

Where will it all end? Roman Catholicism constantly changes and conformity to its surroundings is the rule. Rather than losing certain peoples, she permits customs and pagan and Satanic practices to be incorporated into the area church. Haiti, where voodoo, witch doctors and Satanic practices occur daily, is a country of 99 per cent practicing followers of Roman Catholicism.

Some scholars have found that 75 per cent of the rites and ceremonies of the Roman Catholic Church are of pagan origin.

It is not at all unusual in the light of past Biblical prophetic events that today's happenings could bring another part of God's time calendar to completion. For a further understanding of the divisions of Rome and the Common Market, it is recommended that the inquisitive student of eschatology read with understanding the books of Daniel, Ezekiel, Joel, Zechariah and Revelation and other inspired books on this timely topic.

Let it be said at this juncture that it would be completely unfair to dogmatically declare the Romish church of today to be the embryonic world church. Other possibilities do exist. We will present them also.

Some noted Bible scholars say that Mystery Babylon is the United States of America. The nation has churches on practically every street corner and is supposedly a Christian nation. Also a nation full of sin and immorality would certainly fill the bill, especially with a movement to unite all churches into one religious entity.

The United States of America, everyone knows, is the leading nation of the world. Even though she has received a black eye on occasions, she is still the giant with whom kings of the earth and merchants have dined. Her grandeur in almost every conceivable area has had global significance, influence and impact. As the melting pot of many nations, including those of ancient Rome, she also is a nation of pleasure seekers who are teetering on a Sodom and Gomorrah-like destruction. Just as Lot was carried away by the angels before destruction came, even so the rapture may evidence the same.

Lastly in making an analysis of world events, conditions and statistics in light of what the Bible reveals, it should also be noted that the emergence of the authentic Babylon of old is not entirely ruled out. It is not necessary that reconstruction occur on the ashes of the original site literally. The ancient city of

Nebuchadnezzar on the Euphrates River was and still is located on a very strategic piece of real estate. Iran (old Persia), Iraq, Saudi Arabia, Syria, Kuwait, Jordan and Yemen are a confederation of Arabic nations surrounding this site. Most of these Muslim nations, although often bickering with each other, are part of an oil cartel, mostly members of OPEC. It is undeniable that they hold an economic grip on the kings of this world, with the abundance of that much needed commodity, black gold (oil). It is estimated that two-thirds of the world's known oil reserves are in the Middle East. Consumption of oil has risen in Western Europe, Japan and the United States. Along with this the Islamic religious system is expanding at an alarming rate. There are not too many places in the world where Islam does not touch. Certainly the Antichrist is at work in the Ayatollahs. See how the masses of people are controlled and manipulated with a snap of their fingers.

In this chapter three possibilities have been presented as to the identity of the coming world church. The possibilities have in no way been exhaustive. Other things might develop which are still unforeseen and far removed from anything thus far discussed. From time to time people step out on a limb, saying they know for sure who will be the beast of the world church. Names like Henry Kissinger, David Rockefeller, or even the pope and others have been suggested. Some people look with a pointed finger of suspicion at anyone who does not measure up to their expectations. At this point in time it really does not matter if the man of sin has even been born yet or not. The major emphasis is not on the Antichrist and his identity, but the world system which is being prepared for him to take over on that appointed day.

The Apostle John wondered in great admiration at the harlot world church in his vision of the end time days (Revelation 17:6-7). Readers of this book may be wondering also and saying can these things really be? If you are in an apostate church now, a United church connected to the World Council of Churches, it could be that this book has accomplished its purpose in drawing you to a strong, steadfast, separated, fundamental, Bible-believing, soul winning church where you can become active in serving your blessed redeemer His way.

9

The Destruction of the World Church

The Harlot (Mystery Babylon), the World Super Church headed by Antichrist, will meet her demise much quicker than she had her development. She has been developing for centuries of time but in one hour she will be burnt to a cinder.

Revelation 18:8-10 reveals that *"she shall be utterly burned with fire: for strong is the Lord God who judgeth her. And the Kings of the earth, who have committed fornication and lived deliciously with her, shall bewail her burning. Standing afar off for the fear of her torment, saying. Alas, alas, that great city Babylon, that mighty city! for in one hour is thy judgment come."* (Vs. 19), *"And they cast dust on their heads, and cried, weeping and wailing, saying. Alas, alas, that great city, wherein were made rich all that had ships in the sea by reason of her costliness! for in one hour is she made desolate."*

Beyond a doubt the fire of destruction will inundate the city of whoredom in one hour. Whether it is a sixty-minute time period or longer makes no difference. What does matter, though, is that it will be swift.

Remember, when these prophetical statements were written by the Apostle John there were no nuclear weapons, no missiles, no advanced technology or anything John might be able to relate to with eye contact. If you lived in John's day, how would you describe an airplane, helicopter, tank, cannon, nuclear explosion, interstellar space flight, or any number of modern twentieth century phenomena? John's terminology in no way does injustice to a literal interpretation of the Bible or inspiration of the very words.

Preachers of years gone by who believed in the imminent return of Christ at the rapture immediately followed by a tribulation period, could only speculate to the internal evidence given in the Bible on phrases and words that we of a latter day might relate to in a different way. Islands and mountains fleeing away, hundred pound hail stones, a sea of glass mingled with fire, fire proceeding out of their mouths, breastplates like fire, horses with heads that look like a lion's head and who issued fire and smoke out of their mouths. Many, many terms such as these were somewhat more profound mysteries which were of course believed by faith. It is not so strange that God used natural occurrences to bring about His will and plan. His will is the whole story of history. Remember, life itself is a supernatural event. God is responsible for every snowflake that falls from heaven, every blade of grass in the meadows and every grain of sand upon the seashore. Surely *"by Him all things consist and have their substance"* (Colossians 1:17, 18). When people begin to understand their God and His sovereignty, they will begin to understand His comprehensive plan in relationship to their lives.

Before we continue to describe the destruction of the world church, it would do well to go into a little background information of the way we use the word "church." The word for church in the Greek is ekklesia, a contraction of two Greek words, ek (out of) and klesia (to call), or (to call out of). A church is a called out-group, assembly, or congregation. It is used in the Bible in various ways. In the political sense, it is an assembly *"called out from the populace"* (Acts 19:32, 39, 41), as a Jewish assembly *"called out from the land of Egypt"* (Acts 7:38), and most commonly of the church of Jesus Christ and the New Testament *"called out from the world"—"...thou art Peter, and upon this rock I will build my church"* (Matthew 16:18).

The coming world church will be a political and religious assembly of peoples from the world who give their allegiance to the Antichrist. This assembly, a global congregation, will be compelled to receive an identification mark. It will be the number six, six, six. It will be engrafted in some fashion on the right hand or the foreheads of the adherents. This mark will be the I.D. card of existence. Revelation 13:16-17 relates this fact plainly: *"And he causeth all, both small and great, rich and poor, free and bond, to receive a mark in their right hand, or in their foreheads: And that no man might buy or sell, except he that had the mark, or the name of the beast, or the number of his name."*

The beast, as we have seen in Revelation 17:4 has the whore church riding on his back, meaning he is carrying her or controlling her. Through his position of prominence among the inhabitants of the world and his global influence, he is able to carry it off. Those in his apostate church will all have the mark. If one refuses, he will surely face imprisonment or execution, Revelation 6:9-11.

The harlot church will have her heyday, but she will also have her payday. She will receive the just recompense of her rewards. As for the beast, the man of sin, what is to become of him? The Word of God gives us the answer. With his empire crumbling about him, he erects his image in the rebuilt temple bringing an abomination of desolation to the Jews. During this time the emphasis is primarily centered around God's elect people, Israel, but with worldwide ramifications. Matthew 24:15 states:

"When ye therefore shall see the abomination of desolation, spoken of by Daniel the prophet, stand in the holy place, (whosoever readeth, let him understand:)" (Verse 21), *"For then shall be great tribulation, such as was not since the beginning of the world to this time, no, nor ever shall be."* (Verse 22), *"And except those days should be shortened, there should no flesh be saved: but for the elect's sake those days shall be shortened."*

With many of his followers still intact, Antichrist prepares to do battle with even the armies of God, Revelation 19:19. In what manner this occurs is not really clear. To be sure, the battle is the Lord's. Make no mistake about that. Revelation 19:11 tells us that the armies of heaven will be following the King of Kings and Lord of Lords (also Revelation 19:16). The impending confrontation will take place on a vast triangular plain, 15 x 15 x 20 miles, northwest of Jerusalem called Esdraelon at Megiddo (Armageddon). When Napoleon viewed this plain he commented that all the battles of all times could have been fought here simultaneously. It is here that the ultimate victory of victories takes place. Jesus Christ returns to earth to execute judgment as He brings in His millennial kingdom, Revelation 19:15.

The fate of the beast is sealed. Read the following with understanding. *"And I saw the beast, and the kings of the earth, and their armies, gather together to make war against him that sat on the horse, and against his army. And the beast was taken, and with him the false prophet that deceived them that had received the mark of the beast, and them that worshipped his image. These both were cast alive into a lake of fire burning with brimstone."* (Revelation 19:19,20)

Coincidently, the Second Coming of Christ is the deciding factor in the bringing in of righteousness and the defeating of the Satanically controlled world church of Antichrist.

A thousand years of peace and perfect harmony and tranquility commences with our Lord Jesus reigning upon David's throne with a rod of iron (Psalms 2:9 and Revelation 19:15). During this time Satan is bound in the bottomless pit. Think of a world without a Satanic influence. With Satan bound and Christ ruling, what a world that will be. For those of us who have been living in a sin-scourged world, this will be heaven on earth. Although the culprit of this subject was tossed bodily into the lake of fire, this in no way means annihilation. For those who would teach a cessation of existence, soul sleep, or annihilation the following amazing verse declares otherwise: *"And the devil that deceived them was cast into the lake of fire and brimstone, where the beast and the false prophet are, and shall be tormented day and night for ever and ever."* (Revelation 20:10)

We say it is an amazing verse because it shows that after one thousand years of time have elapsed, the beast and the false prophet are still in the lake of fire with a conscious awareness and with real torment of body and soul which will last for all eternity.

This is certainly an ugly picture. There is nothing great in it to behold. The evil power of misery and destruction will glory in her majestic reign but it will only be for a short duration. The final and ultimate victory will be the Lord's: *"Vengeance belongeth unto me, I will recompense, saith the Lord. And again, The Lord shall judge his people. It is a fearful thing to fall into the hands of the living God."* (Hebrews 10:30, 31).

10
The Destiny of the Beast's Company

This book would not be complete if we did not acknowledge the fate of Antichrist's company and all the unsaved of all nations who actually live through the tribulation period. Although billions will perish during the holocaust, other billions will survive in some fashion. In their natural bodies these billions will be standing on the threshold of a millennial kingdom. Will they be permitted to enter and share as partakers of the glory of the Lamb? Will there be compassion or condemnation for the rejecters of Christ and the followers of the beast?

There will evidently be three classes of people on the earth at that day. They are intermingled upon the earth. They will have to be separated one from another. (Matthew 13:30). Husbands and wives will be torn asunder. Mothers and daughters, fathers and sons, sisters and brothers will all be required to stand in the appropriate line of judgment. For some this will be the glorious day of liberation and freedom, a day of wonderful rejoicing. For others it will be a time of shame, agony, despair and punishment.

Most folks who read Matthew 24 become enamored with the content, especially with the gruesome detail spelled out so graphically of those tribulation years. It is there that they many times stop and ponder the subject matter. The fact of the matter is, it does not stop at Matthew 24, but continues into chapter 25:31-46. In these verses we find the survivors of the tribulation. They are being divided up into various classifications. The omniscient eyes of Jesus Christ are now penetrating hearts and minds. All will stand without excuse and with stopped mouths before the only all-righteous judge. Matthew 25:31-34 says: *"When the Son of man shall come in his glory, and all the holy angels with him, then shall he sit upon the throne of his glory. And before him shall be gathered all the nations: and he shall separate them one from another, as a shepherd divideth his sheep from the goats. And he shall set the sheep on his right hand, but the goats on the left. Then shall the king say unto them on his right hand. Come, ye blessed of my Father, inherit the kingdom prepared for you from the foundation of the world."*

It is clear and without controversy that two lines will be established—the right line is for the saved gentiles or sheep and the left line for the goats, the unsaved gentiles of the nations. No Jew will be in these lines. This judgment is primarily for the gentile nations. To get a proper grip on this entire situation, one must compare scripture with scripture, by inductively drawing from God's word, and the whole process of events will become crystal clear.

As one indeed puts verse upon verse, the whole account will begin to hit home. The reality and cruciality of that day is still at least seven years away.

Joel 3:2 adds more light: *"I will also gather all nations, and will bring them down into the valley of Jehoshaphat, and will judge them there for my people and for my heritage Israel, whom they have scattered among the nations, and parted my land."*

There will be no appeals. All will stand in silence waiting for the verdict to be handed down. Then the sentence will be administered by the eternal righteous Judge and King, Jesus Christ. Matthew 25:41-46 tells us what will happen to the guilty: *"Then shall he say also unto them on the left hand, depart from me, ye cursed, into everlasting fire, prepared for the devil and his angels:... And these shall go away into everlasting punishment: but the righteous into life eternal."*

(NOTE: This is not the Great White Throne Judgment at the end of time. That judgment is still at least one thousand and seven years future.)

Countless millions of Jews and gentiles will come to the saving knowledge of Jesus Christ as Saviour and true Messiah during the tribulation. Revelation 7:4-8 tells us the exact number—one hundred forty four thousand (144,000) from each tribe of Israel. God undoubtedly knows the tribal ancestry of the Jews of today, although the Jews themselves have lost contact with their family tree. Romans 11:26 tells us that *"All Israel shall be saved."* This does not mean every single Jew circumcised physically, but those circumcised in heart. The Apostle Paul says *"For we are the circumcision...and have no confidence in the flesh"* (Philippians 3:3).

Thus all Israel will be saved corporately as a nation of believers. Also along with the Tribulation Jews, there will be a multitude of Gentiles who will embrace Christ at this time. Something not spoken of often is the fact that there will be a great revival taking place on the earth. This will be occurring amidst the persecution of Antichrist and his secret service of those days. Some say that revivals often break out during great hours and times of distress and trial.

Revelation 7:9, 14 shows that this will be the case of those who find Christ during days of turmoil and grief: *"After this I beheld, and, lo, a great multitude, which no man could number, of all nations, and kindreds, and people, and tongues, stood before the throne, and before the Lamb, clothed with white robes, and palms in their hands;… These are they who came out of great tribulation, and have washed their robes, and made them white in the blood of the Lamb."*

There we have it, the sheep and goats, saved and unsaved gentiles who have survived the tribulation. We have mentioned the other group already but not by her group name. The word "brethren" designates this special group of people as found in the context of Matthew 25:40. This portion of scripture describes certain sheep who give shelter, food, clothing and water to a group called brethren.

There is no problem in determining the ones called "brethren". For those who remember or know history about Nazi Germany, recall the genocide of the Jews. A story like "The Diary of Anne Frank" is more than just a story. It is an actual real life and death account of a Jewish family sheltered, fed, clothed and cared for in secret. A day of similar circumstance lies ahead just around the bend of the road. Instead of Hitler's Gestapo, it will be the Antichrist's militant henchmen who will hunt out and seek to destroy Israel or all in collaboration with her. Those sheltered and given protection in tribulation days will be Jews or brethren. Those providing the same will be the sheep.

My friends, the vital question of concern which you might be deliberating over is not so much to what group you might belong but how you might escape this time altogether. Well meaning Christians who hold to a different eschatological view say that all Christians should be prepared for the tribulation. Some who have experienced concentration camps of Nazi Germany attest to this fact. Surely tribulation has always been the fate of all true believers and rightly so, but not the Great Tribulation period. Jesus declares that all those who stand by Him will to some extent experience persecution. John 15:18-21 states: *"If the world hate you, ye know that it hated me before it hated you. If ye were of the world, the world would love his own: but because ye are not of the world, but I have chosen you out of the world, therefore the world hatest you… If they have persecuted me, they will also persecute you."*

And also in John 16:33b Jesus again tells us: *"…In the world ye shall have tribulation: but be of good cheer; I have overcome the world."*

Will there be tribulation for the Christian? Yes: but not the tribulation! That time of judgment and wrath is reserved for the ungodly and will make all other times of tribulation seem like a Sunday School picnic in comparison.

Read some supporting scriptural reasons why the true body of believers in Christ will not experience this time of wrath:

1. Revelation 19:7 says that all born again believers are the bride of Christ. (Would you honestly permit your bride to experience wrath?)

2. Colossians 2:17-27, Ephesians 1:22, 23, 3:1-6 says that we are part of the body of Christ. (Would wrath come upon Christ's own body?)

3. I Thessalonians 1:10 & 5:9 says that Christians are not appointed to wrath, nor will they go through the "Day of the Lord."

4. Titus 2:13 says Christians are looking for the "Blessed Hope" which is the glorious appearing of the great God and Savior Jesus Christ. (What kind of Blessed Hope would that be if one has to go through the Great Tribulation first?)

5. Revelation 6-19 finds no mention of the Church, because they are not on earth, but have been raptured to heaven.

6. Revelation 3:10 says there is no condemnation to those who are in Christ Jesus.

7. Revelation 3:10 says believers will be "*kept from the hour of temptation which will come upon the whole world.*"

8. Philippians 3:20 says that our citizenship is in heaven not earth.

9. 2 Thessalonians 2:7 says the Holy Spirit who indwells believers who in turn hold back corruption will be taken out of the way. (If he goes, believers go.)

10. Jeremiah 30:7 says that the tribulation is for the Jews, Time of Jacob's Trouble.

11. Isaiah 26:20—a time of indignation for Jews.

12. Daniel 9:24 states the seventieth week is determined for thy people (Jews).

These plus many more verses support the fact that a rapture of the body of Christ is truly imminent.

(NOTE: Israel and the Church of Jesus Christ are separate entities. J. Dwight Pentecost in this book "Things to Come" makes reference to this fact:

"...the church could not have been in view in this or any other Old Testament prophecy. Since the church did not have its existence until after the death of Christ (Ephesians 5:25-26), until after the resurrection of Christ (Romans 4:25; Colossians 3:1-3), until after the ascension (Ephesians 1:19-20), and until after the descent of the Holy Spirit at Pentecost with the inception of all His ministries to the believer (Acts 2), the church could not have been in the first sixty-nine weeks of this prophecy. Since it had no part in the first sixty-nine weeks, which are related only to God's program for Israel, it can have no part in the seventieth week, which is again related to God's program for Israel after the mystery program for the church has been concluded."[10]

Be a part of the true church now, the body of Christ. Be ready for the rapture so you may completely escape this time of wrath and judgment. Receive Christ today. Do not give any assistance to those who are trying to establish unity without doctrine, a world church in embryonic form.

11
The Demarcation Lines Must Be Drawn

Christians must take a stand. We cannot be idle, while the rest of the world advances on their relentless journey of perdition. At this time it is imperative that lines be drawn, lines of demarcation. The Random House College Dictionary says that demarcation means:

(1) the determining and marking off of the boundaries of something, 2) separation by distinct boundaries. Both of these definitions are quite appropriate. In light of this, the faithful followers of Christ, who are living fundamental, separated lives must draw this line individually. It is not a geographical location but rather a relative one. The line of defense might exist with one's own church, associates or household.

Romans 16:17-18b tells us: *"Now I beseech you, brethren, mark them who cause divisions and offenses contrary to the doctrine which ye have learned;...by good words and fair speeches deceive the hearts of the simple...and avoid them."*

Often internal squabbling among believers breaks out. This should not be tolerated or have any place in the church. Trivial skirmishes have often accelerated into major disruptions in congregations. This often culminates in splits and the ruination of local churches. Most internal difficulty can be averted by avoiding the formation of cliques and factions, while developing spiritual maturity, prayer, fellowship and love. Remember dissension is a tool of the devil.

As hurtful as this internal strife among believers might be, a much more menacing form of dissension is external discord and contention. Strong lines of defense must be established. External influences can exert tremendous pressure upon pastors and their stand on separation. Many ministerial associations have controlling influences in towns. Hospitals, radio stations, local governments and public schools identify with these interdenominational ministerial organizations. Other churches may label you as legalistic, fanatical or just plain too stiff. This makes for a difficult outreach because the word gets around so quickly and your church becomes marked and labeled. This happens to anyone who takes a stand for Christ—so expect it!

This writer is not simply riding a hobbyhorse. The facts are cut and dried and throughout this book have been clearly presented. If the defense of the faith breaks down now, expect the hour of reckoning to arrive. Thank God, many lines of demarcation have been set up over the years which have proved to be strong bulwarks of spiritual might.

Organizations have come into being also for the express purpose of setting up lines of demarcation. The American Council of Christian Churches is one which also takes a vitally strong position in counteracting the goals of the World Council and the National Council of Churches. As necessary as these groups are, they only put a dent in the framework of apostasy and the formation of the one world church.

The question that every informed Christian should ask himself is just where do I draw the line of demarcation myself? How far can I go in my relations with certain peoples and groups who might welcome individuals into their camp simply because they call themselves Christians? Review the Biblical teachings on separation as you ponder the support of interdenominational and non-denominational groups, who are taking the one-world church course.

Christians have always held to high moral ethics and standards. Because certain cults and isms are in agreement and are moral also, is this grounds for agreement when doctrine is lacking? This is serious business. If the one-world church is to be filled with church people, then church people had better be scrutinized to see which side they are really on.

12
The Disintegration of the Bible

When I was first saved and began to learn of prophecy and end-time events, someone shared with me the exploits of the anti-Christ as stated in Revelation 13:7-9: *"And it was given unto him to make war with the saints, and to overcome them: and power was given him over all kindreds, and tongues, and nations. And all that dwell upon the earth shall worship him, whose names are not written in the book of life of the Lamb slain from the foundation of the world. If any man have an ear, let him hear."*

This one who will control the masses of humanity will somehow have to jettison the true Word of God if he is to assume the position that he is God—2 Thessalonians 2:4 *"Who opposeth and exalteth himself above all that is called God, or that is worshipped; so that he as God sitteth in the temple of God, shewing himself that he is God."* I thought to myself, "How could this guy pull this off, knowing that God's Word will never pass away?" Psalms 119:152 *"Concerning thy testimonies, I have known of old that thou hast founded them for ever."* Isaiah 40:8 *"The grass withereth, the flower fadeth: but the word of our God shall stand for ever."* Matthew 5:18 *"For verily I say unto you, Till heaven and earth pass, one jot or one tittle shall in no wise pass from the law, till all be fulfilled."* Matthew 24:35 *"Heaven and earth shall pass away, but my words shall not pass away."* 1 Peter 1:25 *"For verily I say unto you, Till heaven and earth pass, one jot or one tittle shall in no wise pass from the law, till all be fulfilled."* Satan, however, has always disputed God's Word. He began right in the Garden of Eden when he said to Eve *"...ye shalt not surely die..."* Genesis 3:1-5. And he continued down through the centuries of time, including the dark ages when the Roman Catholic Church placed the Bible on the "Index" (a list of books forbidden to be read by the laity, apart from interpretation of Holy Mother Church).

But Protestants say they will not be snookered again. We are educated now. We are aware of Satan's tactics. We have read 2 Corinthians 2:11 *"Lest Satan should get an advantage of us: for we are not ignorant of his devices."*

Oh really! Satan does not do things in one fell swoop. He operates in lukewarm waters. If all the Bibles were immediately confiscated, total opposition and a cry would emanate from the Christian community. When the Bibles change gradually, however, little by little people get adjusted and acclimated to new surroundings, structures and situations—even scriptures. It's like the frog in the pot. This is exactly what has happened and is still happening even among staunch advocates of the true Bible (KJV). Some of the finest preachers have shifted over to the new copyrighted Bibles—NIV, gender neutral Bibles, new age versions. Satan operates in Religion. The more the merrier. Apostate religions and cults have sent more people to a Christless eternity than all the sin pleasures combined. Yes Satan comes as an angel of light, performing miracles and deceiving if possible the very elect. Some very important Bible verses are:

Matthew 24:24 *"For there shall arise false Christs, and false prophets, and shall shew great signs and wonders; insomuch that, if it were possible, they shall deceive the very elect."*

2 Corinthians 11:3, 4 *"But I fear, lest by any means, as the serpent beguiled Eve through his subtlety, so your minds should be corrupted from the simplicity that is in Christ. For if he that cometh preacheth another Jesus, whom we have not preached, or if ye receive another spirit, which ye have not received, or another gospel, which ye have not accepted, ye might well bear with him."*

2 Corinthians 11:13-15 *"For such are false apostles, deceitful workers, transforming themselves into the apostles of Christ. And no marvel; for Satan himself is transformed into an angel of light. Therefore it is no great thing if his ministers also be transformed as the ministers of righteousness; whose end shall be according to their works."*

Let me share with you a story: While ministering as a Pastor in north central Pennsylvania in the 1980's, our Independent Pastoral Fellowship met with a man passing through our area who shared with us pastors (13 in all) some incredible things which I had never heard before. His name was Dr. David Otis Fuller—a great saint of God and a true champion of the preservation of the King James Bible versus the soon-to-come-out new versions. After Dr. Fuller's presentation, several key and crucial things burned at my heart:

1. Why change the Bible?

2. Is not changing, tampering with, adding to or taking away from the Bible forbidden? The following verses are very clear:

Deuteronomy 4:2 *"Ye shall not add unto the word which I command you, neither shall ye diminish ought from it, that ye may keep the commandments of the LORD your God which I command you."*

Proverbs 30:5-6 *"Every word of God is pure: he is a shield unto them that put their trust in him. Add thou not unto his words, lest he reprove thee, and thou be found a liar."*

Revelation 22:18, 19 *"For I testify unto every man that heareth the words of the prophecy of this book, If any man shall add unto these things, God shall add unto him the plagues that are written in this book: And if any man shall take away from the words of the book of this prophecy, God shall take away his part out of the book of life, and out of the holy city, and from the things which are written in this book."*

3. If the Bible I use and preach from is wrong and needs updating, what have I and millions of others been using all these years?

4. What about Bible Preservation?

With this newfound information, I began to diligently search, study and scrutinize any material I could get my hands on. To my discovery, I found that the debacle we now find ourselves in is not really new or novel. I found that the Apostle Paul was directly confronting the issue while visiting with a group of men in Athens, Greece—Acts 17:16-21. These men were Epicureans, Stoicks, and Gnostic philosophers who denied the Deity of Christ, believed that all material and bodily things were evil, that the planets have souls, that there was no heaven or hell, and a whole slew of other apostate views. These men were in a direct lineage from where our modern cults and Bible-altering ideas spring. You see, the same rationale was espoused by some in the Christian faith. While the apostles were still alive, these heresies could be acted upon and squelched.

But, not long after the passing of the foundational apostles and the completion of the canon, certain of these devious wolves began to get into the business of teaching their unholy precepts on a larger scale. Jude 4 *"For there are certain men crept in unawares, who were before of old ordained to this condemnation, ungodly men, turning the grace of our God into lasciviousness, and denying the only Lord God, and our Lord Jesus Christ."*

Some of the early church fathers who are still quoted for many of their writings were actually pawns in Satan's long reaching plans. Men like Clement of Alexandria (Egypt) who in 200 AD founded a school dedicated to Bible translation along heretical lines, followed by star pupils such as Origin (185-254 AD) followed by Eusebius (260-340 AD) who introduced and injected apocryphal writings and myths. The translating and production of corrupted scriptures in Alexandria was well underway and things began to fall into place and became worse and worse. These men began to alter God's Word, eventually eliminating thousands of words and entire Bible verses. In spite of this, the catechetical school at Alexandria became accepted by modern scholarship as a center of Christian learning.

Now comes a most crucial moment in time. In 330 AD, Constantine the Emperor of Rome claimed to have had a conversion experience and consequently stopped all Christian persecution and embraced Christianity. The first thing he did was to order Bibles from Alexandria—of all places.

Fifty Bibles were ordered by Constantine inscribed on the finest vellum (animal skins), none of which survived the centuries of time. One of these, however, is supposedly in the archives of Rome. It was used by Jerome to produce a Latin version in 382 AD called the Vulgate. From this source came all Roman Catholic Bibles.

While all this was going on, thousands upon thousands of true Bibles were being produced by dedicated scribes and Jewish Masorites. These men were meticulous in their copying. If one mistake was encountered, the whole text was discarded and eventually destroyed. This source material from the original languages throughout the Grecian world and Europe (Byzantine world 452-1453 AD) preserved the true line of Scripture. Remember, all of this was being done without a printing press. None of these earlier copies survived. The earliest ones we have date to approximately 900 AD. Thousands of them have survived from this time. They all compare favorably with each other.

When King James wanted a Bible in English, he and his finest scholars used these texts call The Received Text or Textus Receptus. The Bible which would be called the King James Bible of 1611 or the Authorized Text is the Bible of the Reformation Church and used by saints and missionaries in carrying the Gospel message to a world lost in sin. This was not an easy endeavor as much blood was shed and havoc was wrought at the hands of Rome, i.e. The Inquisition.

This short chapter in this book is at best an overview. I would suggest that you read the research of many gifted and devoted people who are indeed holding a strong defense for God's true Bible, the KJV.

I would be remiss if I did not include some background information on the development of the corrupt Bibles that are now fully hitting the market today.

At the end of the nineteenth century a Russian explorer, Count Tischendorf, went on an expedition to Mt. Sinai. At its base was a monastery. He noticed some discarded scrolls in a trashcan. Inquisitively he examined them and found them to be very old. Although they were tattered and worn, smudged and erased, Tischendorf thought perhaps there was some value to his find. These manuscripts would eventually come to be called "Sinaiticus, or the Alexandrinus "Aleph". These portions of unholy writ were taken back to Russia and today rest in a museum. The Sinaiticus and Vaticanus disagreed with each other extensively. Yet no matter, because of their antiquity (300-360 AD) they became classic because they were closer to the Apostolic era than the Masoritic texts in Hebrew (500-1000 AD) and Byzantine texts in Greek.

Now comes the greatest degree of damage. Time had gone by—centuries in fact. The Reformation, the great schism in Rome, the discovery of America, the invention of the printing press had all come about in God's perfect timing. Satan and his notorious plan were not about to end. All of his plans would not go for naught.

Satan had entered into the hearts of two prominent men, namely Brooke Foss Westcott (1825-1903) and Fenton John Anthony Hort (1828-1892). In 1881 they published their Introduction to the New Testament in which they endeavored to justify the reconstruction of the New Testament text on the basis of the corrupt Vaticanus "B" and Sinaiticus "Aleph". They offered the theory that the original New Testament text had survived in the two oldest manuscripts. (Note: Whenever you see a marginal foot saying "not included in oldest manuscripts" it is referring to these two).

Liberals embraced it as the very latest in the "science" of New Testament textual criticism. The Greek text that they produced was to become the basis of the Revised Version of 1881. This new Bible would be initially rejected by most mainline churches of that day. Remember though, the "frog in the pot." A little leaven leaveneth the whole lump. The ancient seed had germinated. Much could be said about Westcott and Hort being Satan worshippers who offered devotions to the Blessed Mother. Here we see the doctrinal sentiments of the two men who entered the English New Testament Revision Committee and dominated it during the ten years required to produce the Revised Standard Version.

Since that time until now, revision committee after revision committee have formed to give us supposedly more accurate Bibles. The criterion in each case is easy readability. Nothing could be further from the truth. The King James Bible of 1611 was the prime reader of school children during the early years of America. In fact, it was esteemed highly until the McGuffy Reader came into use.

Here is a list of the most popular perverted versions, all with copyrights and money to be made:

Holman Christian Standard
New International
New American Standard
Revised Standard
New Revised Standard
New Century Version
The Living Bible (Good News for Modern Man)

Watch out for the coming of the gender neutral and New Age Bibles.

If you have been using an NIV, I will give you an exercise. Please look up the following verses and see if they are there. If not, why not? Remember, tampering with God's true word is forbidden and great consequences will follow as stated in Revelation 22:18-19.

Matthew 17:21
Matthew 18:11
Matthew 23:14
Mark 7:16
Mark 9:44 and 46
Mark 11:26
Mark 15:28
Luke 17:36
Luke 23:17
John 5:4
Acts 8:37
Acts 15:34
Acts 24:7
Acts 28:29
Romans 16:24

In this above list, sixteen are whole verses omitted. Many other portions are altered, deleted in part, or paraphrased. Many things dealing with the blood, Deity of Christ, His return, and other doctrinal areas are omitted. Note about the NIV: In 1 Timothy 3:16 "God was manifest in the flesh" is taken out of the verse and it is altered to read "he appeared in a body." The word *God* (Gk. Theos) is eliminated. Thus a reader may ask "Who is the *he* that appeared in a body?" The cults love this rendering.

It is my hope that your appetite for truth has been whetted and you might understand the urgency of these last days. The embryonic world church is forming rapidly. Please read on, as the next chapter is also critical in Satan's exploits in paving the way for the man of sin.

13
The Debacle of Cloning

Since this chapter deals with cloning and its connection with end-time events, I will include a definition at the outset.

Clone

NOUN, **1.** A cell, group of cells, or organism that are descended from and genetically identical to a single common ancestor, such as a bacterial colony whose members arose from a single original cell.

2. An organism descended asexually from a single ancestor, such as a plant produced by layering or a polyp produced by budding.

3. A DNA sequence, such as a gene, which is transferred from one organism to another and replicated by genetic engineering techniques.

4. One that copies or closely resembles another, as in appearance or function: *"filled with business-school clones in gray and blue suits"* (Michael M. Thomas).

TRANSITIVE VERB, **1.** To make multiple identical copies of (a DNA sequence). **2.** To create or propagate (an organism) from a clone cell: *clone a sheep*.**3.** To reproduce or propagate asexually: *clone a plant variety*.**4.** To produce a copy of; imitate closely: "*The look has been cloned into cliché*" (Cathleen McGuigan). American Heritage Dictionary, Fourth Edition

Of primary concern is the noun form as stated in number 3 above and the verb form number 2 above.

In order to understand how and why we of this modern era find ourselves pondering the benefits and ethics of cloning, we need to go back to the beginning of the underlying cause and purpose of this debacle and dilemma. If you are diligent and have a searching mind for truth, you will discover at least in part the unfolding of the mysteries of the ages. God's eternal plan has been etched on the opening pages of scripture. In capsule form we have before us the reason for the universal deluge of Noah's day and the unfolding of last time events. The Bible has not changed. Bible scholars have pondered the opening chapters of Genesis only to pull back in dismay at the possibilities presented in this work. For various reasons, be it peer pressure, faulty exegesis, or a fright to venture into uncharted territories, many schools and institutions have refrained from speaking forth in classrooms and pulpits the subject matter you are about to examine.

To put it in basic terms, God has a unique plan. Every minute detail is woven into the prophetic structure of the scriptures. We will see this in types, images, shadows, numbers, even in cryptic and allegorical form.

Give this book a chance. It may change your preconceived ideas and any prejudices you harbor. Remember one thing at the outset. Prophecy is sure, yet the finished out workings of the details become clear after the fact. Nothing will thwart God's plan, stay His hand or alter His design. Satan has attempted too, but even he becomes a pawn in God's grand chessboard of time and eternity.

Let us go back 4500 years to a pre-flood world filled with wickedness and evil imaginations and thoughts of the depraved descendents of Adam's race. In Genesis 6:5 we read "*And GOD saw that the wickedness of man was great in the earth, and that every imagination of the thoughts of his heart was only evil continually.*"

Most people think that God destroyed mankind in the global deluge of Noah's day simply because they were bad and sinful. That is certainly true. But all mankind are sinful and totally depraved to this very day as shown in Romans 5:12 "*Wherefore, as by one man sin entered into the world, and death by sin; and so death passed upon all men, for that all have sinned:*" The evil which required extermination of the human race must have been unique and astronomical. This particular evil and wickedness I believe has to do with an insidious and relentless plan of Satan. If you read very careful what I am about to share, you will be astounded. Men have been bad and evil throughout history. Jeremiah 17:9 "*The heart is deceitful above all things, and desperately wicked: who can know it?*"

There is much more, I believe, than meets eye at first glance.

Over in Matthew 24:37 we read: "*But as the days of Noe were, so shall also the coming of the Son of man be.*" The Lord's return to earth seems to hinge upon this prophetic statement. Let us analyze it more fully. Just what was going on during Noah's day? Look at Genesis 6:1-4. Verse one tells us that men began to multiply on the face of the earth. Indeed they did. A very conservative estimate of the antediluvian population would be six billion people at the time of the flood. This is based on various factors as longevity, family size, time span (almost 1700 years) from Adam to the flood and an exponential growth rate. It is interesting to note that our present population is estimated to be six billion people worldwide. Remember as it was in the days of Noah. Six is also the number of man. It has also been 6000 years since Adam's creation or six thousand-year days.

Secondly verse 2 tells us "*That the sons of God saw the daughters of men that they were fair; and they took them wives* (plural) *of all which they chose.*" The traditional view of this verse is that the sons of God were of the godly line of Seth. This would, however, imply that Seth's lineage was uncorrupted (godly) and did not mingle or marry with either the sons of Cain or any that had populated the earth for 1600 plus years. Genesis 5:4 "*And the days of Adam after he had begotten Seth were eight hundred years: and he begat sons and daughters:*" Surely they did not live in isolated villages with walls. The wheat and tares grow together. Jesus said in Matthew 13:38 "*...but the tares are the children of the wicked one*"

There must be some other explanation as to whom these sons of God might be. It does not say anywhere that Seth's lineage was godly, although some were, i.e. Enoch and Noah. The Bible speaks of the sons of God in various ways. The descendents of Seth also drowned in the flood of humanity.

The book of Job, for instance, says in Job 1:6 "*Now there was a day when the sons of God came to present themselves before the LORD, and Satan came also among them.*" The same thing is found in Job 2:1. Over in Job 38:4-7 we read "*...all the sons of God shouted for joy...*" when God created the earth. Clearly these sons of God were angelic beings. Angels also appear as men in many places throughout scripture (i.e. at the birth of Jesus, at His tomb, at His ascension). Some may have even entertained angels unawares—Hebrews 13:2.

Now you may be asking yourselves: Does not the Bible say that angels neither marry, nor are given in marriage? (Matthew 22:30 and Mark 12:25) Yes it does say that angels do not procreate or marry. But you must know of assuredly that the sons of God spoken of in Genesis 6 who took wives of all whom they chose were fallen angels who had left their own habitation (natural estate). Jude speaks on this in verse 6: "*And the angels which kept not their first estate, but left their own habitation, he hath reserved in everlasting chains under darkness unto the judgment of the great day.*" And verse 7 tells us: "*Even as Sodom and Gomorrah, and the cities about them in like manner, giving themselves over to fornication, and going after strange flesh,….*" These fallen angels apparently were doing the same things as the people in Sodom and Gomorrah. These fallen sons of God were employed by Satan to genetically corrupt the bloodline of humanity. Why, you may ask? The answer I believe is found in Genesis 3:15 concerning a Messiah Redeemer who would come through the seed of a woman. "*And I will put enmity between thee and the woman, and between thy seed and her seed; it shall bruise thy head, and thou shalt bruise his heel.*" Galatians 4:4 reads: "*But when the fullness of the time was come, God sent forth his Son, made of a woman, made under the law,*"

Although Genesis 3:15 speaks of the seed of a woman, it does not clearly state a virgin birth but it is most surely implied. This Messiah Redeemer would come from the seed of a woman, not the seed of a man as shown in Luke 1:34: "*Then said Mary unto the angel, How shall this be, seeing I know not a man?*" You see, our sin nature is passed down through the masculine lineage through the propagation of both male and female seeds. Jesus Christ, however, had no human father. That holy one born to Mary was the only begotten Son of God (John 3:16). Mary became pregnant through the operation of the Holy Spirit as told in Luke 1:35: "*And the angel answered and said unto her, The Holy Ghost shall come upon thee, and the power of the Highest shall overshadow thee: therefore also that holy thing which shall be born of thee shall be called the Son of God.*"There were only two men who came into this world pure, sinless and undefiled whose father was God: Adam and Jesus Christ—the last Adam. 1 Corinthians 15:45-47: "*And so it is written, The first man Adam was made a living soul; the last Adam was made a quickening spirit. Howbeit that was not first which is spiritual, but that which is natural; and afterward that which is spiritual. The first man is of the earth, earthy: the second man is the Lord from heaven.*"

Satan surely did not want the Messiah to come and he almost succeeded by contaminating the genetic composition of mankind.

Overwhelming Biblical evidence seems to support this view. Peter also writes in chronological order concerning this. Note: 2 Peter 2:4-6: "*For if God spared not the angels that sinned, but cast them down to hell, and delivered them into chains of darkness, to be reserved unto judgment; And spared not the old world, but saved Noah the eighth person, a preacher of righteousness, bringing in the flood upon the world of the ungodly; And turning the cities of Sodom and Gomorrah into ashes condemned them with an overthrow, making them an ensample unto those that after should live ungodly;*"The extermination of contaminated humanity is directly related to the fallen angels cohabiting with women.

Yes, Noah and his family were spared because they were not corrupted by the intermarriages of the sons of God and daughters of men. Genesis 6:9 tells us that Noah was a just man and perfect in his generations. This does not mean Noah was sinless, but does mean not contaminated genetically. He and his family carried in their genes the potential human race from whence would come our savior.

There is more, however, when we inductively compare and rightly divide the Word of Truth. The next verse, Genesis 6:4, speaks of "giants in the earth in those days." The word for giant is the Hebrew word Nephileem, which means "fallen ones"—surely not the jolly green giant or Goliath. This verse also continues telling that this cohabitation between the fallen sons of God (Nephileems) and daughters of men produced a mutant race of half-angelic, half human beings. The wording says the offspring born became mighty men—Arcons (titans), men of renown. I believe these mighty ones built the pyramids with mathematical brilliance and precision and other phenomenal structures and were also the source of Greek mythology (i.e. Zeus, Neptune, Hercules, etc. etc.) Another whole book could be written on this topic.

Now with all of this background information, how does this tie into end-time events? We all know about Dolly the sheep—and the cloning of monkeys, mice, and dogs—even sterile mules. Do not be surprised if one day you hear that a human being has been cloned. One cult says this has already happened.

A friend of mine was telling me that it might be possible to clone a human from some ancient genetic material. He suggested that some dried blood from the Shroud of Turin might be used to produce a cloned Jesus if it is authentic. This would be sacrilegious in every way. But if it happens, we would see an unholy virgin birth bringing forth an Antichrist. We may be closer than you think.

Remember as it was in the days of Noah. Legislation is now underway which would allow cloning from embryonic blood from a mother's umbilical cord. The hope is that things like regenerated nerve tissue would restore paralytic patients to full mobility. Diseases such as Alzheimer's, even cancer, might be eliminated. Even the reversal of the aging process could be possible. With such a need, the enthusiasm and push for cloning will no doubt become a common reality in the very near future. To the natural mind, the fountain of youth is attainable.

Along with all of this, I make mention of the abundance of the UFO phenomena. Many independent studies suggest a strong connection with alien abductions. These unprompted people relayed facts of examination of their reproductive parts by their abductors. The events seem to coincide. The descriptive terminology of grayish, large-eyed creatures in vivid detail could not have been staged or rehearsed by those creditable sources. Prominent people, airplane pilots, public officials, common housewives to name a few seek no notoriety and often put their jobs and careers on the line.

Television shows and motion pictures seem to be preparing humanity to accept as commonplace our encounter with aliens. Although many do not put credence in these shows and sightings and consider them entertainment and out of this world, they still provoke an acceptance and at least a subliminal acknowledgment of their existence. Crop circles, sightings, and reports stir man's imaginations.

Make no doubt about it though. The Bible does speak about fallen angels as "...principalities, powers, rulers of the darkness of this world..." Ephesians 6:12. Satan is called "the prince of the power of the air." Ephesians 2:2. Ezekiel seems to describe some sort of space vehicles, while in other places craft as flaming chariots transport people away.

If all this does tie into Satan's continuing plan to alter the genetic code of mankind, you might expect more activity in this realm. I cannot but think that the millions upon millions of dollars spent for space exploration (probes to Mars and other planets, space stations, solar telescopes, etc.) have an urgency tied into them. Whether secretive or top secretive, the agenda to venture into these dark corners are upon us.

Every chapter in this book has been written to show that the Embryonic World Church is hatching. Please read and share this book.

14
The Debauchery of Sodom

A crucial aspect relating to end time events and formation of "The Embryonic World Church" is the infiltration of homosexual activity as an alternative lifestyle with acceptance into mainstream churches. We have seen reports of the ordination of openly gay priests and an installation of a gay bishop in the Anglican Church and the issuance of marriage licenses to both lesbian and gay partners in San Francisco, and the flaunting of gay participants in parades and demonstrations across our nation.

Many years ago I read in Luke's Gospel, chapter 17:28, that the sinful activities in Lot's day in Sodom would be indicative of events just prior to Christ's second coming. I had a hard time trying to visualize this coming about. In my lifetime, however, this prophecy is literally being unfolded and fulfilled.

There is absolutely no doubt that it is an abomination for a man to lie with a man or a woman to lie with a woman. Liberal theologians say they find no conflict with Sodomite practices and espouse the practice openly. Certain new Bibles even take the word Sodomite out of the text.

This chapter is not written as an afterthought but as an integral unfolding of a world and church ripe for judgment. A Biblical journey is in order to develop this theme. You could read newsprint and watch TV reports, mostly from a prejudicial stance and liberal slant on this topic. But the bottom line is what does the Bible say? Let us check out some verses:

Note: Romans 1:24-28 *"Wherefore God also gave them up to uncleanness through the lists of their own hearts, to dishonour their own bodies between themselves:*

Who changed the truth of God into a lie, and worshipped and served the creature more than the Creator; who is blessed forever. Amen.

For this cause God gave them up unto vile affections: for even their women did change the natural use into that which is against nature:

And likewise also the men, leaving the natural use of the woman, burned in their lust one toward another; men with men working that which is unseemly, and receiving in themselves that recompense of their error which was meet.

And even as they did not like to retain God in their knowledge, God gave them over to a reprobate mind, to do those things which are not convenient:"

In other words God washed His omnipotent hands of these Sodomite abominations. Abomination? Yes, indeed. Leviticus 18:22 reads: *"Thou shalt not lie with mankind, as with womankind: it is abomination."*

Verses 24-25 continue: *"Defile not ye yourselves in any of these things: for in all these the nations are defiled which I cast out before you: And the land is defiled: therefore I do visit the iniquity thereof upon it, and the land itself vomiteth out her inhabitants."* (Read the rest of the chapter.)

We used to talk about this with a blush on our faces. In hushed tones we speedily read past these verses. Well, we cannot exclude what God intends for us to be understood any longer. How clear can it be? The scriptures are explicit.

They (homosexuals) call it coming out of the closet. They say they were born with these tendencies and cannot help themselves. They say society should not squelch their desires, for it might harm their psyche. There is one excuse after another. Legislators and judges pander them and their cause for votes and political gain. Of a surety, the land will vomit out the inhabitants thereof. Could our good old USA be approaching its last days before it is flushed down the sewer of degradation?

When churches and church leaders accept and tolerate gay marriage and rites, or even ordain gay clergy, who "preach" their ungodly rationale and precepts to a slumbering audience, the end cannot be far off and may be at the doorsteps already.

We live in a world today where even Boy Scout leaders are gay, camping with young boys under the stars, perhaps initiating and indoctrinating unsuspecting boys to an ungodly lifestyle from which there is no escape without Jesus Christ. So whom do they blame? The Boy Scouts, of course.

Folks, be alert, be informed. Preachers, Sunday School teachers, church members, educate one another. Share your knowledge and pray for those who espouse homosexuality in these last days.

15
The Deluge of the Nile

I have attempted to weave into this book a series of end-time events. Although not necessarily in chronological order, you will find direct ties which dovetail and touch each other prophetically in completing God's plan for the culmination of this age.

The world's furniture is now in place, the table has been set, and ancient prophecies are about to unfold. This is history in advance.

One thing that sets Bible prophecy apart from other predictors and prognosticators is that the God-inspired writers were 100% accurate in what they penned. With this in mind and with a Bible in hand, search with me and find the frightening and vivid descriptions of an impending devastation and complete demolition of two key spots of Satanic activity—namely Egypt and Damascus, Syria.

Both of these countries are haters of Jewry. Terrorists and radical Islamic insurgents are supported by these regimes directly or indirectly. From suicide bombers to the military might of Hamas, Al Qaeda, and Hezbollah, these stone-throwing and rocket-launching fanatics wish to see God's people Israel annihilated from the earth. But that will never happen. Israel is the apple of God's eye (Zechariah 2:8). The Abrahamic promise is still in effect (Genesis 12:1-3). All the antics of Satan will be thwarted. "*Vengeance is mine; I will repay, saith the Lord.*" Romans 12:19. If I might say so reverently, looking into Scripture is like looking into a heavenly crystal ball.

A very graphic description of sure to come events is given in Ezekiel's prophecies (Ezekiel 29) which I will analyze shortly. Since time immemorial the Nile River has meandered on a northern course in Egypt for some 500 miles. It is literally the life blood of a nation. It has been the umbilical cord which brought nourishment, grandeur and greatness to a people—witness the pyramids and other ancient monuments and edifices. With its annual springtime flooding the banks became well irrigated and rich fertile soil deposits along its pathway helped provide abundant crops in an arid and dessert climate.

History itself shows Egypt's influence on the world. Even with its blessings, the Pharaohs of time past and Presidents of the present have despised Jewish people and would desire their demise. God's hand, however, has been their protectorate. Remember the Exodus of some two million people under Moses' guidance. The story is all too well known to us. The rest of the story, however, has yet to be told.

Now getting back to Ezekiel, I will pick out critical and sensitive portions for you. It is necessary, however, for you to read chapters 29 and 30 to get the full picture. Follow along with me as I describe the following verses:

Chapter 29:

Verse 3—Shows the arrogant pride of Pharaoh motivated and controlled by the great dragon (Satan). "...*Thus saith the Lord God; Behold, I am against thee, Pharaoh king of Egypt, the great dragon that lieth in the midst of his rivers, which hath said, My river is mine own, and I have made it for myself."* cf Revelation 12:19.

Verse 4—Shows that something is about to come that will devastate the land and the booming fishing industry; literally the stench of rotting fish having been deposited after being washed up onto the banks by a surge of water and now decaying in the hot sun. "*...I will cause the fish of thy rivers to stick unto thy scales, and I will bring thee up out of the midst of thy rivers, and all the fish of thy rivers shall stick unto thy scales.*"

Verse 5—Shows some event is going to cause men, fish, and beasts to be thrown into the open fields. Their dead carcasses are being devoured by the fowl scavengers. "*And I will leave thee thrown into the wilderness, thee and all the fish of thy rivers: thou shalt fall upon the open fields; thou shalt not be brought together, nor gathered: I have given thee for meat to the beasts of the field and to the fowls of the heaven.*"

Verse 9—Shows the outcome of this event. "*And the land of Egypt shall be desolate and waste...*"

Verse 10—Shows the extent of this desolation. "*...from the tower of Syene even unto the border of Ethiopia.*" (Note the map for these locations.)

This has not yet happened. So where does all this fit in concerning end-time events? When Ezekiel wrote, there was not a great dam located at a place called Syene (Today's Aswan). Only a tower was noted at this location. This gives us a precise geographical location which positions the Aswan Dam at this spot. Amazing!

Today this great dam, built with Russian engineering and expertise in the 1960's, holds back an enormous volume of water creating Lake Nasser which is 310 miles long and six miles wide. Presently the release of water is constant and the controlled outflow is steady. There is no annual flooding or overflowing of the banks.

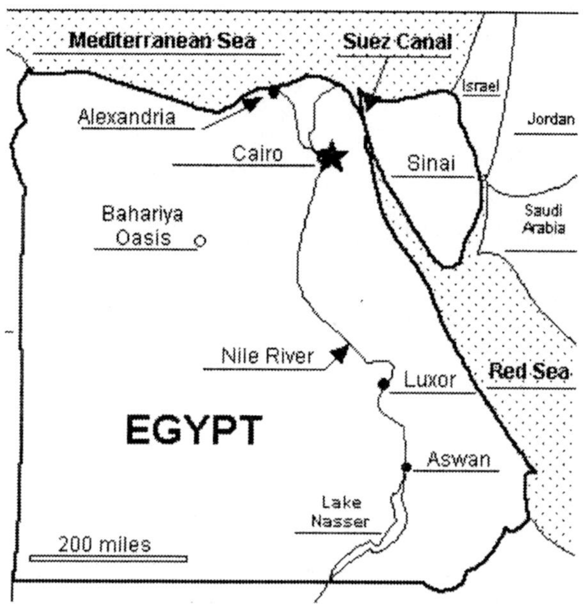

Aswan High Dam from Nasa Satellite

Lake Nasser from Aswan High Dam

The question which immediately comes to mind is: What if this massive dam breaks? Imagine the surge of water cascading northward, inundating every village, town and city from Aswan to the great delta (Tongue of the Nile). It would make the tsunami of 2004 in the Indian Ocean seem like a splash in a puddle in comparison. The populace in the millions will be swept clean. The onward rush would offer very little time to seek high ground or evade the oncoming onslaught.

Verses 11-13—Tell us that it will take forty years for this country to recover as it will remain uninhabitable for this period of time. "*No foot of man shall pass through it, nor foot of beast shall pass through it, neither shall it be inhabited forty years….I will scatter the Egyptians among the nations, and will disperse them through the countries….*"

What could cause the Aswan Dam to fracture and fail? Perhaps an earthquake? Or perhaps a nuclear explosion hitting this target? A small suitcase-size device would do the trick.

Chapter 30: 6-8—Tell us it will occur by means of the sword (warfare) and continues to describe an unleashing of fire in Egypt.

This sounds more like a nuclear device of some kind being detonated rather than an earthquake. It is a well-known fact that Israel has a formidable Army, Navy and Air Force. She is well able to defend herself. No doubt with her back against the wall she will not hesitate to use her full armament. With Israel's back against the Mediterranean Sea, she will have no recourse but to fully defend her small piece of real estate. "*...from the tower of Syene shall they fall in it by the sword, saith the Lord God.*" "*...when I have set a fire in Egypt...*"

The prophet Isaiah also speaks on this very thing. Isaiah 11:15 declares that this mighty surge of water will inundate the entire delta (tongue) seven streams of Egypt. "*And the Lord shall utterly destroy the tongue of the Egyptian sea; and with his mighty wind shall he shake his hand over the river, and shall smite the seven streams...*" Amos 8:8 also tells of this great deluge (flood of Egypt).

Note: When more than one reference is listed in Scripture, it is sure to be noticed with a sense of urgency.

To the inquisitive student of prophecy, I must make mention that the world is not sitting idly by during this time. Watch the total picture.

Continuing in Ezekiel 38, the prophet tells of a great invading force, an axis of Islamic nations advancing upon Israel. Ezekiel 38:1-9 lists the countries by name. Although many bear their ancient names (i.e. Persia = Iran) (Gomer=Germany) (Togarmah=Turkey), they can readily be identified. This invasion will occur, I believe, immediately after the flood of Egypt. Please notice the absence of two key nations in the listing: Egypt and Syria.

We already know why Egypt is not included. But what about Syria? The prophet Isaiah (Isaiah 17:1) said that Damascus, Syria, shall be rendered a rubble heap. This has never occurred in its entire history. Damascus is the oldest continually occupied city on the earth. This is an event of the latter days. Ezekiel 38:16: "*...thou shall come up against my people of Israel, as a cloud to cover the land; it shall be in the latter days...*" With these two nations now gone, the battle resumes. But God intervenes even here, and completes the battle (Ezekiel 38:21-23). The carnage will be so complete that it will take seven years to bury the dead and gather the weapons.

You may have wondered why I included this chapter in this book. I believe the answer is obvious. The Antichrist will have clear sailing to bring in his world church after these invading forces are neutralized.

16
The Doctrines Denied

We now come to the final chapter of this book; a chapter that I believe glues all the issues discussed into one concept—namely idolatry, whether it is of man, or money, material or means. The cause is the result of knowingly or unknowingly distorting or denying doctrine. If doctrine goes, all is lost. Directly or indirectly this is what this book is all about. Doctrine is the most vital area in scripture. The word itself is used over forty times in the Bible. The crucial doctrines of the faith, i.e. the virgin birth, deity of Christ, bodily resurrection, blood atonement, are major and must be embraced without question. Other areas such as ecclesiology and eschatology may have certain gray areas that have been much debated throughout the church age. Readers of this book may hold to any number of last-time events (pre mil, pre trib, post trib, a mil, etc.) yet have no effect on their salvation. Readers may attend different denominations and churches even among the same denominations with splits and still be saved.

The question one must finally deal with as he or she grows in God's grace is one of knowing God as He reveals Himself and His eternal plan. Included in God's plan are the "Doctrines of Grace," all of which are based upon His eternal decree which He purposed in Himself—Eph. 1:11 "*In whom also we have obtained an inheritance, being predestinated according to the purpose of him who worketh all things after the counsel of his own will.*" As one discovers in the Bible God's absolute sovereignty, one must finally bow to a God who knows and controls every aspect of His creation—Colossians 1:16-17 "*For by him were all things created, that are in heaven, and that are in earth, visible and invisible, whether they be thrones, or dominions, or principalities, or powers: all things were created by him, and for him: And he is before all things, and by him all things consist.*" God is aware of every blade of grass, grain of sand, snowflake, star of the sky, hair on your head, every molecule and every atom. He is aware and in control of every dimension of time and space. It is with this we must say Amen and Amen.

The world has humanized God as the man upstairs. In fact man has made himself god—Romans 1:25 "*Who changed the truth of God into a lie, and worshipped and served the creature more than the Creator, who is blessed for ever. Amen.*" Ultimately the man of sin will say he is God—2 Thessalonians 2:4 "*Who opposeth and exalteth himself above all that is called God, or that is worshipped; so that he as God sitteth in the temple of God, shewing himself that he is God.*"

Mankind wants dominance, authority and control. By his very nature man is selfish and self-centered. He wants to do it his way, even in salvation. We have seen the results in history past and present.

I could quote hundreds of scripture portions which deal with His attributes and who God is, but great men have written well and extensively on this subject.

People want a say in the matter, even in salvation. This is humanism at its worst. Man wants some of the credit whether it be the works of his hands, rituals, walking an aisle, even baptism.

They miss God's grace entirely. Two Bible verses that bring it to our attention are: Titus 3:5 "*Not by works of righteousness which we have done, but according to his mercy he saved us, by the washing of regeneration, and renewing of the Holy Ghost*" and Ephesians 2:8, 9 "*For by grace are ye saved through faith; and that not of yourselves: it is the gift of God: Not of works, lest any man should boast.*"

One thing that I notice is that people, preachers and pastors use the term "accept" Jesus as your savior. They certainly mean well. However, "accept Jesus" is not used anywhere in God's Word. The word "receive" is used—John 1:12-13 "*But as many as received him, to them gave he power to become the sons of God, even to them that believe on his name: Which were born, not of blood, nor of the will of the flesh, nor of the will of man, but of God.*" The fact is, God does the accepting. He accepts all of His elect, Ephesians 1:6 "*To the praise of the glory of his grace, wherein he hath made us accepted in the beloved*" and 2 Corinthians 5:9 "*Wherefore we labour, that, whether present or absent, we may be accepted of him.*" He (God) does not sit idly by in heaven twiddling His omnipotent thumbs waiting for us to cast the deciding vote. Bound up in His omniscience and eternal decree is His sovereign grace. He cannot do wrong. When you finally bow to God as the creator, sustainer, controller and Lord, you will be on the right Biblical course.

A question you might ask yourself is: What did I have to say about my physical birth, my gender, personality, height and stature, intelligence, family born into, name, location of birth, color of hair, eyes, skin, etc.? Quite obviously the answer is nothing.

(Note Jeremiah 1:5 "*Before I formed thee in the belly I knew thee; and before thou camest forth out of the womb I sanctified thee, and I ordained thee a prophet unto the nations.*" and Galatians 1:15 "*But when it pleased God, who separated me from my mother's womb, and called me by his grace.*") God placed you into time at exactly the point of His choosing. "*He removeth Kings and setteth up Kings...*" Daniel 2:21 and "*Woe unto him that striveth with his Maker! Let the potsherd strive with the potsherds of the earth. Shall the clay say to him that fashioneth it, What makest thou? or thy work, He hath no hands?*

"*Woe unto him that saith unto his father, What begettest thou? or to the woman, What hast thou brought forth?*" Isaiah 45:9-10. You are God's workmanship, Eph. 2:10 "*For we are his workmanship, created in Christ Jesus unto good works, which God hath before ordained that we should walk in them.*" Not vice versa.

We come into this world dead in sin and must be born again and not one of us seeks after God, Romans 3:11 "*There is none that understandeth, there is none that seeketh after God.*" God, in fact, breaks the gap by His eternal love and purpose, Ephesians 1:4-5, 9 "*According as he hath chosen us in him before the foundation of the world, that we should be holy and without blame before him in love: Having predestinated us unto the adoption of children by Jesus Christ to himself, according to the good pleasure of his will, verse 9*

Having made known unto us the mystery of his will, according to his good pleasure which he hath purposed in himself." Salvation is God's will, not man's will, John 1:13 "*Which were born, not of blood, nor of the will of the flesh, nor of the will of man, but of God.*" Salvation is of the Lord, Psalm 3:8 "*Salvation belongeth unto the LORD: thy blessing is upon thy people.*" and Jonah 2:9 "*But I will sacrifice unto thee with the voice of thanksgiving; I will pay that that I have vowed. Salvation is of the LORD.*"

Many times over scripture is misquoted or taken out of context. One very upsetting portion is found in 2 Peter 3:9 "*The Lord is not slack concerning his promise, as some men count slackness; but is longsuffering to* **us-ward**, *not willing that any should* **perish**, *but that all should come to repentance.*

NOTE: When the words "us" or "we" are used, it refers to the Saints (saved people). What is taken out of context in the above verse is "not willing that any should perish." This does not mean, as some state, that God is not willing that any of mankind without exception should perish. If this were the case, all would be saved. Nothing can thwart God's will. So, they say, all men will be saved. This is universalistic teaching. If God is not willing that all mankind will not perish, why do some perish? So something is wrong with God's will. To be precise here, the "any" refers to the "us-ward" (underlined above). The saints to whom Peter is referring are the "us-ward"—all that the Father gave to Jesus, John 6:37 *"All that the Father giveth me shall come to me; and him that cometh to me I will in no wise cast out."*

If any doubt still exists, the Apostle John states it most eloquently as to who will never perish:

The words of Jesus in John 10:27-29: "*My sheep hear my voice, and I know them, and they follow me: and I give unto them eternal life; and they shall never* **perish**, *neither shall any man pluck them out of my hand. My Father, which gave them me, is greater than all; and no man is able to pluck them out of my Father's hand.*"

Lastly, connected to this, John 6:39 states concerning God's will, that only those who are sheep of the fold will never perish: "*And this is the Father's will which hath sent me, that of all which he hath given me I should lose nothing, but should raise it up again at the last day.*"

It is true that John 3:16 says *"For God so loved the world."* Yet in John 17:9, Jesus says *"I pray not for the world, but for them which thou hast given me…"* Something seems amiss here, but when viewed in its entirety it all makes sense. It is unfair to rip apart verses at one's convenience to make them conform to already assumed notions. The word "world" refers to more than Jews, John 1:11 *"He came unto his own, and his own received him not."* Jesus came to save His people from their sins—Matthew 1:21. He came on a mission and succeeded completely. At the same time we are admonished to preach the Gospel to every creature—Mark 16:15. Why? Because in the world of men God's elect mingle. You see, the wheat and tares grow together. We preach the Gospel, however, to every creature. Otherwise it would be an illegitimate offer.

God has given us the responsibility to reach the lost sheep. John 10:14-16 *"I am the good shepherd, and know my sheep, and am known of mine. 15 As the Father knoweth me, even so know I the Father: and I lay down my life for the sheep. 16 And other sheep I have, which are not of this fold: them also I must bring, and they shall hear my voice; and there shall be one fold, and one shepherd."* I make mention of one more thing. The blood of Christ is sufficient for every one of Adams's race, but efficient for those who believe.

Before I close this section and end this book, there is one more item that has been misconstrued. Namely, a thing called Hyper-Calvinism. To state it briefly, a hyper-Calvinist says if God has it all worked out in advance, we should just sit back and let the world take its course. Those who believe in the absolute sovereignty of God would never take that unbiblical approach. Calvinism is not wrong, but hyper-Calvinism is wrong. All throughout this book the responsibility and defense the saints have in serving our Blessed Lord and Savior have been stated.

Put all of the chapters together now. See for yourself the brevity of time. I would hope and pray that the effort put into this book would not return void, but accomplish a great purpose for God. Share this book. Use it for study and reference. Perhaps you or your loved ones may come to know Jesus as your absolute Lord, King and Savior.

What has been written is hard to accept for many people. When a person wants some say in the matter, they will have difficulty here. With this mentality and faulty exegesis of scriptural doctrines, the man of sin will enter in. The true church will be decimated and a world which receives an altered Bible, miracle men, and false doctrine will suffer the vengeance of our eternal and sovereign Lord and Savior.

Conclusion

Folks, this book is not sheer fabrication, speculation or fantasy. What has been rendered under the various headings all falls into the spectrum of reality. The subject matter is indeed timely and of the utmost importance. The Bible has been consulted and quoted often as our only infallible guide and sourcebook. The world around us has been surveyed as the stage on which Satan and mankind are acting out their roles during the course of time called history. The final curtain is about to descend, bringing a close to the last chapter of the great plan for the ages.

Act 1 opened on creation day and not long afterward Satan began his relentless exploits. As the father of lies, he deceived and has been deceiving mankind ever since the fall. Adam and Eve succumbed to the serpent's insidious meddling. With the entrance of sin, Satan gained a foothold in the affairs of men, molding and manipulating them in their state of spiritual blindness. He almost succeeded in corrupting the whole human race in the days of Noah. Had it not been for the intervention of almighty God, Satan may have succeeded.

Satan is compelled by his very nature to do the things he does.

Failure does not stop him. He has not given up, and will continue to pursue the pathway of destruction until his ultimate collapse in the eternal lake of fire.

Almighty God chose to save His elect from the clutches of the tyrant of tyrants. He will continue to do so until the final curtain comes down. Noah, Abraham, a Hebrew nation, and the saints of Jesus Christ have all overcome the evil one. You can, too.

Christian friend, do not help Satan to bring about his global takeover of the masses. He has enough unsaved people to accomplish his exploits. Satan knows the Bible and can quote passages at length. He certainly knows that his time is running out. This is why he is working overtime, stalking this world like a roaring lion, *"seeking whom he may devour,"* 1 Peter 5:8.

Religion has been Satan's favorite commodity of deception. Every age has seen peoples of various races and creeds following in his wake. Religion has sent more people to hell than all the other sin pleasures combined. Since Cain and Able presented their offerings before God until this present day, the world has, like Cain, chosen to pursue the form of worship that would seem pleasing to man and not God. The heathen who bow before the sun, totem poles, statues and idols are all religious people. The innate knowledge of a god of some sort is in every person. Unfortunately, they turn from the true God *"to man, birds, four-footed beasts and creeping things"* (Romans 1:23). Someday soon they will be worshipping the very man of sin himself as the one true God. Being religious will never get anyone to heaven.

Mankind still continues the same patterns. The search goes on, but it is a search of blindness. The grandeur of a religious system is an attractive force. There is quite a contrast between the edifices of man and the secret hiding places of hidden catacombs where the early Christians worshipped the true God in spirit and in truth. It makes one wonder what went wrong.

Reader, it is our hope that the content of this book strikes home a resounding note and triggers a response that would cause an awakening and re-evaluation of your church and your life. At the same time it must be noted that the Christian is not to give up hope, believing the world is crumbling all about him. Although the days ahead will be bleak and dismal for most of humanity, the future will usher in eternal bliss and glorious rejoicing in the very presence of our Lord and Saviour, Jesus Christ. For those saved and sealed by the

Holy Spirit of God the ultimate hope is in the return of the Lord to rescue his people from the wrath to come. A Bible verse that I lean heavily upon is found in Titus 2:13: *"Looking for that blessed hope, and the glorious appearing of the great God and our Saviour Jesus Christ."* The basic premise contained in this verse of scripture would be hope indeed. If regenerated believers were to go through this time of tribulation what kind of "blessed hope" would that be? We, as born again believers are looking for the rapture, that is the "blessed hope" not the tribulation.

It may be that your friends, relatives and neighbors are on the road of religiosity. They may be lovely people, sincere people, church people and yet people who are unknowingly promoting the formation of a world super church in its embryonic stage of development. They may be in compliance with the World and National Council of Churches or ecumenical or charismatic movements thinking that this is the only way to go.

If conviction has come into your heart through the Holy Spirit, may we exhort you to find a good Bible-believing, Bible-preaching, fundamental, separated, Christ-centered church and there serve Jesus in these critical last days.

Notes

1. Ernest Pickering, "Biblical Separation" (Schaumburg: Regular Baptist Press, 1979), p.154.

2. Merril C. Tenney, general editor, "The Zondervan Pictorial Bible Dictionary" (Grand Rapids: Zondervan Publishing House, 1963), p. 232.

3. John L. Benson, "Who is the Antichrist?" (Schaumburg: Regular Baptist Press, 1978), pp. 16-17.

4. Lorain Boettner, "Roman Catholicism" (Philadelphia: The Presbyterian and Reformed Publishing Company, 1962), p. 141.

5. Ernest Pickering, "The Biblical Doctrine of Separation" (Clarks Summit: Baptist Bible College of Pa., n.d.), pp. 8 & 9.

6. Dr. Mark Jackson, "Ready, Set, Grow" (Clarks Summit: Baptist Bible College, n.d.), pp. 43 & 44.

7. Funk & Wagnalls New Encyclopedia, Vol. 25, p. 236 (New York:Funk & Wagnalls, Inc., 1972)

8. C.I. Scofield, D.D., Editor, "The New Scofield Reference Bible" (New York: Oxford University Press, 1967), pp. 1369-70.

9. N.W. Hutchings, "The Gospel Truth", (Oklahoma City: Southwest Radio Church, 1978), p. 5.

10. J. Dwight Pentecost, "Things to Come" (Grand Rapids: Zondervan Publishing House, 1958), pp. 195-196.